SCOTLAND INTERNATIONALS
IN THE BLACK & WHITE ERA

BY STEVE FINAN

Archie rode a challenge from football common sense, a swivel of the hips took him past the balance of probability. He nutmegged the normal course of events and then, just as stark reality rushed out to close him down, he chipped the ball over the bounds of possibility and into the net.

■ Scotland v England 1962.

SCOTLAND
INTERNATIONALS
IN THE BLACK & WHITE ERA

BY STEVE FINAN

ISBN 978-1-84535-866-2

First published in Great Britain in 2021 by DC Thomson & Co., Ltd., Meadowsidc, Dundee, DD1 9QJ

To purchase this book visit **www.dcthomsonshop.co.uk**

Or Freephone 0800 318 846 / Overseas customers call +44 1382 575580

Typeset & internal design by Steve Finan.

This book is set in Times New Roman regular/bold/italic 13 point on 15.6 point leading.

COVER/BACK COVER DESIGN | LEON STRACHAN

Introduction: This is what Scottish

IT is the cause that unites all football people in our hard wee country – Scotland's fitba team. Our nation, our colours, our hopes and dreams. There is nothing else, not politics, religion, and certainly not club rivalries, that we all agree on.

This is the latest in the Black & White Era library of books. It is a collection of photos which have, for the most part, lain for decades unloved and unlooked at in newspaper and magazine archives.

Some of the photos are a little bit tattered and torn, I can only apologise for that. It isn't easy finding pristine old photos. Some were never developed from negatives and have suffered damage through exposure to light at the wrong time. But all of them show great players and games. The very best within living memory.

It is shamelessly and deliberately a nostalgia trip. These are the names and games that I remember, that we all remember, from good times that now seem far off – when the sun shone, the drink flowed, and life was good whether we won, lost, drew, or were robbed by bad luck and bad refereeing.

There are photos here that will lift the heart. There are players that will stir awed memories. There are tales of games and campaigns that will make you want to lift your arm to wave a Lion Rampant flag and lift your voice to sing the old battle hymns.

But this is Scotland remember – I wouldn't want to kid you on that all of these pages talk of glories and victories.

There are also photos that will bring back the bitter bile of disappointment, and wistful "if only" feelings of unfulfilled potential. Though I suppose that, as a Scotland supporter, you will probably be prepared for this. You remember what it was like. You were there.

The book covers the years from the war, through the 1950s and '60s, until Ally's Army marched to the confident skirl of the pipes in 1978. A second volume will be required to take the story on into the 1980s and 1990s.

You'll recognise here, I'm sure, the likes of George Young, Bobby Evans, Billy Steel, Lawrie Reilly, Billy Bremner, Jim Baxter, Kenny Dalglish and Archie Gemmill. And then there's The King himself, Denis Law.

We'll also take a peek further back to the days of the chief wizard himself, Hughie Gallacher, whose glory years are now close on a century ago. His incredible legend must never be allowed to die.

This is not a definitive history. It is not intended to

patriotism looks like

be. It is merely an attempt to bring old images and old memories back into the light.

Can I take you back to when you stood on the vast slopes of Hampden in the 1960s or '70s? Pick a game, any game, and think back.

There are lulls in the crowd in all football matches, perhaps when play stops for an injury. There is a low undertone of talk, but little real sound or movement.

But then one voice starts and others join in. Hands are raised above heads to clap. Some point to the sky, emphasising the words with jabs into the air. The Lion Rampants are unfurled and waved, and very quickly everyone around you is singing from the heart.

Do you remember how it felt? Tens of thousands of voices. Because that was, in its purest form, the feeling of patriotism. That was the feeling of what it is to be Scottish. That was the manifestation of pride in your nation.

It seemed little at the time. We experienced it so often. But when you think of it now a lump comes to the throat. We were footsoldiers in the Tartan Army and young. We were the voice of the nation. Our songs and our joy was the famous Hampden Roar, the greatest sound in all of world football.

That's what this book is about.

Lastly, although this is a book that looks back, Scotland fans should take it as inspiration and reason to look forward with optimism.

Scotland has always been good at football. We punch greatly above our weight on the world scene.

The game of football is our game. It was born here. We taught the world to play properly when other nations were thrashing about with a kick-and-rush, half-daft patchwork of scrums and mauls. It was a brawl with a ball.

The Scotch Professors of the early days showed the world what football could be if approached as a game of skill, coordinated moves, and true beauty. Fluid, geometric poetry. Many men thinking as one.

Beautiful football is our invention, our tradition, and our birthright.

There will be good times to come, so recognising the good times of the past, even if just in photos you'll see here, gives us perspective. Seeing what proper football and real footballers looked like will help us recognise these things when we see them next.

And you definitely will see them. We must believe this. A day will come when Scottish football again rules the world.

Steve Finan, 2021

CONTENTS

Foreword, by Denis Law

THERE is no feeling in the world that is better than pulling on a Scotland shirt.

I first played for the senior team in October 1958, at Ninian Park, Cardiff. I was a laddie of 18 and got a goal in a 3-0 win over Wales.

Bill Shankly was my manager at Huddersfield, and Matt Busby was the national manager.

I learned about my call up from a newspaper seller in Huddersfield town centre. He called me over and asked if I'd seen the news in *The Examiner* (the Huddersfield evening paper). It said I had been picked for my country.

I've never been so excited in my life, I hadn't even known I was being considered.

Only 11 players were selected in those days, there were no substitutes. I was in the team! I'd never even played for the Under-23s.

Dave Mackay was the captain that day and his team talk got to me so much that I ran all over the place in the first 10 minutes, I was so fired up.

My goal was a bit lucky, to be honest. The Welsh centre-half headed the ball against my head and it went into the goal. But a goal's a goal!

Two weeks later I played for Scotland again. Against Northern Ireland, at Hampden this time, in an unchanged team from the Wales game.

I'm ashamed to say that I kicked Danny Blanchflower all over the park! Matt Busby had told me that he dictated all their play and that I was to "watch him". I was a fired-up, keen-as-mustard teenage laddie and I got carried away.

I'll never forget that night as it was the first time my mother and father ever saw me play as a professional footballer. Goodness knows what they thought of my wild ways. But that's what playing for your country does to you.

I also look back fondly at all the great players I played with in the Scotland team – Dave Mackay, John White, Billy McNeill, Billy Bremner, Jimmy Johnstone, Jim Baxter, Paddy Crerand, Ian St John, Bobby Evans, Eric Caldow, to name just a few.

It was an honour to be on the field with these men representing the hopes of the Scottish nation.

So I've greatly enjoyed looking at all the old photos in this book. The memories come flooding back. The fantastic backing we used to get at Hampden and Wembley, the iconic games, the great teams we played against

I played my last ever game as a professional footballer against Zaire in the 1974 World Cup, 16 years after my first cap. I gave my all in every one of the 55 games I played, and I know that every player who plays for Scotland will do the same.

Ever since I was a lad growing up in Aberdeen and playing football for Powis Academy and Scotland Schoolboys, I have been a Scotland supporter. I will always be a Scotland supporter.

Denis Law, 2021.

Post-war years

IT was the era of storied Scottish internationals such as big George Young and the ever-determined Bobby Evans, the artistry of Billy Steel and Bobby Collins in the middle of the park, and the forward line firepower of Lawrie Reilly, Billy Liddell and Willie Waddell.

For all the great players in those years, however, our appearances at World Cups were embarrassing.

Switzerland 1954 was the year we took a 7-0 trouncing from Uruguay (see page 48). Sweden 1958 saw us gain one point (from Yugoslavia), lose pitifully to Paraguay, then in typical fashion produce our best performance in the final group game against France.

Although it was all too little too late, and we lost 2-1 anyway (see page 60).

Our record against England was just as uninspiring.

In the 10 Home Internationals, 1950-59, we won just once, a 3-2 victory at Wembley in 1951.

But if all this sounds like it was a dark and difficult time for Scotland, it certainly didn't feel like it.

This was also the era of a massive re-engagement with football after the war. Huge crowds squeezed into grounds and brought great enthusiasm with them.

Scotland games were, for the most part, amazingly well attended and the Hampden Roar was a thing of awesome power.

■ 132,817 attended the 1956 Scotland v England game, only to see the day completely spoiled. See page 36.

THE 1945-46 games were referred to as "Victory Internationals" and don't count as full internationals (caps weren't awarded) because not every player had yet been demobbed from the forces.

However, no one could have persuaded the Scottish public the England game wasn't a real game. More than 138,000 squeezed in to Hampden to see Jimmy Delaney score late in a 1-0 home win.

Three members of the team, the Shaw brothers at full-back and centre-half Frank Brennan, were from the tiny village of Annathill, near Coatbridge.

■ Left: England walk out for the 1946 game. These were the days when a football shirt was a shirt you played football in.

■ Right: The crowd certainly didn't treat the game as if it didn't count. This was one of the most joyous events of the immediate post-war years in Scotland. It was celebrated loudly and at great length.

Team v England, April 13th, 1946:
1. Bobby Brown (Queen's Park)
2. Davie Shaw (Hibernian)
3. Jock Shaw, captain (Rangers)
4. Willie Campbell (Morton)
5. Frank Brennan (Airdrieonians)
6. Jackie Husband (Partick Thistle)
7. Willie Waddell (Rangers)
8. Neil Dougall (Birmingham City)
9. Jimmy Delaney (Manchester United)
10. George Hamilton (Aberdeen)
11. Billy Liddell (Liverpool)

16

■ **Scotland v Ireland 1946. Frank Brennan, newly transferred from Airdrie to Newcastle United, gets the ball clear.**

■ **Team v Ireland, November 27th, 1946:**
1. Bobby Brown (Rangers)
2. George Young (Rangers)
3. Davie Shaw, captain (Hibernian)
4. Willie Campbell (Morton)
5. Frank Brennan (Newcastle United)
6. Hugh Long (Clyde)
7. Gordon Smith (Hibernian)
8. George Hamilton (Aberdeen)
9. Willie Thornton (Rangers)
10. Jimmy Duncanson (Rangers)
11. Billy Liddell (Liverpool)

■ Goalkeeper Bobby Brown, also newly transferred and who would become Scotland manager 21 years later, made his debut that day.

NEWSPAPERS of the day complained that the famous "Hampden Roar" wasn't at its full strength for the England game in 1948, and said the team suffered from a lack of support from the 135,000 crowd. We lost 2-0.

■ **Left: Field Marshal Montgomery salutes the military parade before watching the game.**

■ **Right: In a photo that is showing its age, George Young leans on England and Notts County centre-forward Tommy Lawton.**

■ **Team v England, April 10th 1948:**
1. **Ian Black (Southampton)**
2. **John Govan (Hibernian)**
3. **Davie Shaw (Hibernian)**
4. **Billy Campbell (Morton)**
5. **George Young, captain (Rangers)**
6. **Archie Macaulay (Arsenal)**
7. **Jimmy Delaney (Manchester United)**
8. **Bobby Combe (Hibernian)**
9. **Willie Thornton (Rangers)**
10. **Billy Steel (Derby County)**
11. **Billy Liddell (Liverpool)**

20

■ Two more age-damaged shots from the 1948 Auld Enemy game.
England centre-half Neil Franklin challenges for a high ball with Billy Liddell.

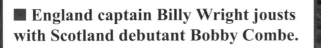
■ **England captain Billy Wright jousts with Scotland debutant Bobby Combe.**

The Rosebery Colours

ARCHIBALD PHILIP PRIMROSE, Lord Rosebery, Liberal Prime Minister 1894-95, was honorary president of the Scottish Football Association, and also honorary president of Heart of Midlothian, around the turn of the 19th to 20th Centuries.

The Scotland team wore his pink and yellow racing colours, instead of the dark blue, several times. The most notable occasion being a 4-1 rout of England in the 1900 Home International at Celtic Park. This was the game in which Queen's Park centre-forward Robert Smyth McColl (Toffee Bob, who went on to set up a chain of sweet shops) scored a hat-trick.

Lord Rosebery, watching from the stand, told captain John Robertson, of Rangers, "I haven't seen my colours so well sported since Ladas won the Derby in 1894", which is a posh boy's way of saying: "Aye! Yiz got right in aboot thum".

Scotland wore the colours on at least nine occasions during Lord Rosebery's lifetime (he died in 1929), and in 1949 and 1951 in games against France. And again in a 2-1 win over Finland in Helsinki in 1954, the last warm-up game before the World Cup in Switzerland.

The SFA again adopted the colours, or a version of them, as the "away" strip from 2014. Fans were less than impressed, with many a reference to Mr Blobby.

Lord Rosebery was the richest Prime Minister in history, with a personal fortune that would amount to around £95 million today. This was mainly due to marrying Hannah de Rothschild, the Rothschild banking dynasty heiress, in 1878.

He donated the Rosebery Charity Cup, played for by East of Scotland clubs to raise money for the Edinburgh Royal Infirmary and Leith Hospital. It ran from 1883 to 1944-45. Hearts won it 32 times, Hibs 22.

■ **Right: George Young, in the Rosebery Colours, leads out Scotland to play France at Hampden in April 1949.**

■ **Team v France, April 27th, 1949:**
1. **Jimmy Cowan (Morton)**
2. **George Young, captain (Rangers)**
3. **Sammy Cox (Rangers)**
4. **Bobby Evans (Celtic)**
5. **Willie Woodburn (Rangers)**
6. **George Aitken (East Fife)**
7. **Willie Waddell (Rangers)**
8. **Willie Thornton (Rangers)**
9. **Billy Houliston (Queen of the South)**
10. **Billy Steel (Derby County)**
11. **Lawrie Reilly (Hibernian)**

SCOTLAND v France again, this time in the Colombes Stadium, Paris, on May 27th, 1950.

The Scots won 1-0, with a commanding performance, built upon the rock-solid Rangers Iron Curtain defence.

The goal came from East Fife inside-forward Allan Brown on 69 minutes. Scotland even had the luxury of a missed Billy Liddell penalty.

Brown was to join Blackpool in December of that year for a then Scottish record fee of £26,000. He went on to have a lengthy playing and managerial career in England. One of his highlights was laying the foundations of the Nottingham Forest team that his successor as Forest manager, Brian Clough, would take to great heights.

He died in 2011, but is surely a contender for the Scottish Football Hall of Fame.

■ **Right: The team that 1950 day was, from left:**
Lawrie Reilly, Hibernian (centre-forward)
Billy Liddell, Liverpool (outside-left)
Billy Steel, Derby County (inside-left)
Allan Brown, East Fife (inside-right)
Bobby Campbell, Chelsea (outside-right)
Willie Woodburn, Rangers (centre-half)
Alex Forbes, Arsenal (left-half)
Ian McColl, Rangers (right-half)
Sammy Cox, Rangers (left-back)
Jimmy Cowan, Morton (goalkeeper)
George Young, Rangers (right-back and captain)

Big George

GEORGE YOUNG, the Rangers colossus, was the best-known Scotland star of the immediate post-war period. He won 53 caps between 1946 and 1957, the first man to make 50 Scotland appearances, captaining the side 48 times. The tally would be higher if it hadn't been for the war – no internationals were played until 1946 when George was already 24.

He was a wide-shouldered, barrel-chested, six-feet-two defender, weighing 15 stones. But George, though a very powerful man and certainly no pushover, was a always a fair player.

In the days before Scotland had a manager George arranged training sessions and travel arrangements for his fellow players and liaised with the shadowy selectors, the SFA committee who picked the team. Some players, especially the Anglo-Scots, complained that George had too much influence on team selection.

The end of his Scotland career was, however, needlessly awkward.

Scotland beat Spain 4-2 at Hampden in May 1957

■ **Left, George with his great friend and fierce rival England captain Billy Wright before the Auld Enemy clash of 1956. It was a 1-1 draw in front of 132,817.**

■ Team v England, April 14th, 1956:
1. Tommy Younger (Hibernian)
2. Alex Parker (Falkirk)
3. John Hewie (Charlton Athletic)
4. Bobby Evans (Celtic)
5. George Young, captain (Rangers)
6. Archie Glen (Aberdeen)
7. Graham Leggatt (Aberdeen)
8. Bobby Johnstone (Man. City)
9. Lawrie Reilly (Hibernian)
10. Ian McMillan (Rangers)
11. Gordon Smith (Hibernian)

in a World Cup Qualifier. Before the return in Madrid a few weeks later, rumours flew that big George was to announce his retirement after a swansong at the Bernabeu.

However, at no point did George say this himself. He was, at all times, an honest, popular man, respected by the fans, his fellow and opposition players, and the press.

There were also rumours about a groin strain as George had sat out a friendly with World Cup holders West Germany the week before the Spain game.

But George had publicly declared himself fit for Madrid and everyone expected the nation's most experienced defender to play.

On the day before the game the chairman of the selectors walked into the hotel dining room and asked Tommy Docherty, who had captained the side in Germany, to gather the next day's players for a team photo. Nothing was said to George, no one told him he wasn't playing.

He was left sitting at his table, openly snubbed in front of the players and the press corps, who referred to it for ever after as "the Madrid incident". Scotland lost 4-1.

George's international career was over. A humiliating end for a man who, until that point, had been regarded as our most venerable player.

■ **Team v Spain, in Madrid, May 26th, 1957:**
1. Tommy Younger (Liverpool)
2. Eric Caldow (Rangers)
3. John Hewie (Charlton)
4. Dave Mackay (Hearts)
5. Bobby Evans (Celtic)
6. Tommy Docherty, captain (Preston North End)
7. Gordon Smith (Hibernian)
8. Bobby Collins (Celtic)
9. Jackie Mudie (Blackpool)
10. Sammy Baird (Rangers)
11. Tommy Ring (Clyde)

■ **Right, George leads out Scotland for a Hampden friendly v Denmark in 1951.**

■ **Team v Denmark, May 12th, 1951:**
1. Jimmy Cowan (Morton)
2. George Young, captain (Rangers)
3. Sammy Cox (Rangers)
4. Jimmy Scoular (Portsmouth)
5. Willie Woodburn (Rangers)
6. Willie Redpath (Motherwell)
7. Willie Waddell (Rangers)
8. Bobby Johnstone (Hibs)
9. Lawrie Reilly (Hibs)
10. Billy Steel (Dundee)
11. Bobby Mitchell (Newcastle)

■ **Bobby Mitchell gets in a shot.**

■ Danish keeper Eigil Nielsen tips a Lawrie Reilly effort over the bar.

■ Nielsen later became famous for inventing a new type of ball, using 32 black and white panels, and no laces. Adidas snapped up the design for their Telstar, which became the official match ball for the 1970 and 1974 World Cups, and made Eigil a very wealthy man.

Playing while injured

FOOTBALL was tough in the 1950s. The laws allowed tackles that the very sight of would cause today's players to spill their macchiato lattes. And we nod our heads and say, "Aye, they were hard men", and agree that the game was better in those days.

But was it?

We might smile to think that the players of today would crumple in the face of the tackles of yesteryear, but physiotherapists and medical teams would be truly horrified.

There were hard knocks in the old days, and the players were truly resolute men. But there were a lot of bad injuries.

The trouble was that clubs (and countries) expected players to play on, injured or not. There are horrific tales of players of the 1950s and '60s given cortisone injections week after week to treat injuries that never got better. Cortisone just masked pain, it didn't treat the problem.

Untold damage was done to tendons and joints that resulted in decades of pain and reduced mobility long after these men gave up playing.

You can always tell if an old bloke was a footballer in his younger days. Look to see if he limps.

■ **Left: Wales captain Alf Sherwood helps Lawrie Reilly hirple off the field during the Scotland 2, Wales 0 Home International of 1955.**

■ **Team v Wales, November 9th, 1955:**
1. **Tommy Younger (Hibernian)**
2. **Alex Parker (Falkirk)**
3. **Joe McDonald (Sunderland)**
4. **Bobby Evans (Celtic)**
5. **George Young, captain (Rangers)**
6. **Doug Cowie (Dundee)**
7. **Gordon Smith (Hibernian)**
8. **Bobby Johnstone (Manchester City)**
9. **Lawrie Reilly (Hibernian)**
10. **Bobby Collins (Celtic)**
11. **John Henderson (Portsmouth)**

THE crowds for 1950s Scotland-England games at Hampden were mind-boggling.

They were:

1950 – 133,300.

1952 – 134,504

1954 – 134,544.

1956 – 132,817.

1958 – 127,874.

The 1952 game is pictured, left.

The ticket price for the highest attendance listed above, 1954, was three shillings (15p).

Adjusted for inflation, the 2021 equivalent of three shillings is about £4.20.

■ **Team v England, April 5th, 1952:**
1. **Bobby Brown (Rangers)**
2. **George Young, captain (Rangers)**
3. **Willie McNaught (Raith Rovers)**
4. **Jimmy Scoular (Portsmouth)**
5. **Willie Woodburn (Rangers)**
6. **Willie Redpath (Motherwell)**
7. **Gordon Smith (Hibernian)**
8. **Bobby Johnstone (Hibernian)**
9. **Lawrie Reilly (Hibernian)**
10. **Ian McMillan (Airdrieonians)**
11. **Billy Liddell (Liverpool)**

THERE was a storm of interest, inspiring a 107,765 crowd, when the USA rolled up to play Scotland for the first time at Hampden in 1952. We'd been used to seeing Americans in movies, but they were a rare and exotic species in the flesh.

Disappointingly, they didn't bring Gary Cooper or Grace Kelly with them (the big Hollywood movie that year was *High Noon*). They didn't bring much football talent either.

Despite the Americans fielding six members of the team that famously thrashed England 1-0 at the World Cup of 1950, we beat them 6-0 – and eased up in the second half after being 4-0 up after half an hour.

■ **USA keeper Frank Borghi, looking not entirely sure where the ball is, and wearing fancy American knee-pads.**

■ **Team v USA, April 30th, 1952:**
1. **Jimmy Cowan (Morton)**
2. **George Young, captain (Rangers)**
3. **Sammy Cox (Rangers)**
4. **Jimmy Scoular (Portsmouth)**
5. **Willie Woodburn (Rangers)**
6. **Hugh Kelly (Blackpool)**
7. **Gordon Smith (Hibernian)**
8. **Ian McMillan (Airdrieonians)**
9. **Lawrie Reilly (Hibernian)**
10. **Allan Brown (Blackpool)**
11. **Billy Liddell (Liverpool)**

SCOTLAND v England 1956. We should have won this one. The Scots were 1-0 up after an hour through a sublime Graham Leggat chip (his trademark method of scoring).

There followed a fantastic half-hour of attacking football from both sides. However, just as the fans were clearing their throats for one of the greatest Hampden roars of all time, up popped Johnny Haynes to score with virtually the last kick.

Leggat would be transferred from Aberdeen to Fulham two years later, where he struck up a prolific goal-scoring partnership with, of all people, Johnny Haynes.

■ **Tommy Younger cuts out a cross in the 1956 game.**

■ **Team v England, April 14th, 1956:**
1. **Tommy Younger (Hibernian)**
2. **Alex Parker (Falkirk)**
3. **John Hewie (Charlton Athletic)**
4. **Bobby Evans (Celtic)**
5. **George Young, captain (Rangers)**
6. **Archie Glen (Aberdeen)**
7. **Graham Leggat (Aberdeen)**
8. **Bobby Johnstone (Manchester City)**
9. **Lawrie Reilly (Hibernian)**
10. **Ian McMillan (Airdrieonians)**
11. **Gordon Smith (Hibernian)**

Hard man to please

BILLY STEEL was a genius, but a hard man to play a game of football with. In an era when a good proportion of training was laps of the pitch, or sprints up terracing steps, Billy would quickly become bored and go off on his own to perform hand-springs and tumbles, then work with a ball.

And he was remarkably self-confident. He knew how good a footballer he was. He could do things with a ball other players wouldn't even think of. Opposition half-backs knew what he could do too, and committed X-rated tackles on him.

What really set Billy apart was his habit of criticising, loudly and personally, flaws in his teammates. He didn't mince words. Tommy Gallacher, his teammate at Dundee FC, had to be held apart from Billy on several occasions.

Billy was unlucky to be the first Scotland international sent off in a 1951 game that became known as "The Battle of Vienna". Scotland lost 4-0 and received brutal treatment.

Late in the game, Steel, always a tigerish tackler, went for a 50-50 with centre-half Ernst Ocwirk that left the Austrian captain doing an extended version of Swan Lake while lying on the turf.

Swiss referee Jean Lutz, possibly a ballet fan, took more notice of these gyrations than the actual fairness of the challenge and Billy received his marching orders.

■ **Team v Austria, December 13th, 1950:**
1. **Jimmy Cowan (Morton)**
2. **George Young, captain (Rangers)**
3. **Willie McNaught (Raith Rovers)**
4. **Bobby Evans (Celtic)**
5. **Willie Woodburn (Rangers)**
6. **Alex Forbes (Arsenal)**
7. **Bobby Collins (Celtic)**
8. **Eddie Turnbull (Hibernian)**
9. **John McPhail (Celtic)**
10. **Billy Steel (Dundee)**
11. **Billy Liddell (Liverpool)**

■ **Billy looks for a rebound in an earlier match against Austria at a frosty Hampden. The negative has been badly light-damaged**

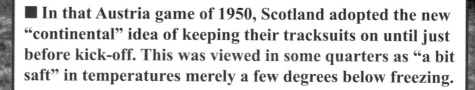

■ In that Austria game of 1950, Scotland adopted the new "continental" idea of keeping their tracksuits on until just before kick-off. This was viewed in some quarters as "a bit saft" in temperatures merely a few degrees below freezing.

■ Billy Steel did everything but score that day, this shot slipping just past the post. A few weeks previously he had been transferred from Derby County to Dundee, for a Scottish record fee of £22,500, just £4,000 short of the world record Preston North End had paid Sheffield Wednesday for Eddie Quigley a year earlier.

SCOTLAND set off for a two-game tour of Scandinavia in the summer of 1952.

They recorded a 2-1 win over Denmark in Copenhagen then lost 3-1 to Sweden in Stockholm, and returned to a hostile press reception (by the standards of the era) for underperforming.

■ **Team v Denmark, May 25th, 1952:**
1. Jimmy Cowan (Morton)
2. George Young, captain (Rangers)
3. Sammy Cox (Rangers)
4. Jimmy Scoular (Portsmouth)
5. Andy Paton (Motherwell)
6. Alex Forbes (Arsenal)
7. Lawrie Reilly (Hibernian)
8. Ian McMillan (Airdrieonians)
9. Willie Thornton (Rangers)
10. Allan Brown (Blackpool)
11. Billy Liddell (Liverpool)

■ **Team v Sweden, May 30th, 1952:**
1. Jimmy Cowan (Morton)
2. George Young, captain (Rangers)
3. Sammy Cox (Rangers)
4. Jimmy Scoular (Portsmouth)
5. Andy Paton (Motherwell)
6. Alex Forbes (Arsenal)
7. Lawrie Reilly (Hibernian)
8. Wilson Humphries (Motherwell)
9. Willie Thornton (Rangers)
10. Allan Brown (Blackpool)
11. Billy Liddell (Liverpool)

EVEN the greatest players on the planet had to take a deep breath at the thought of playing against Scotland in the biggest stadium in the northern hemisphere, with the loudest support in the football world.

Hampden, filled with upwards of 100,000 Scotsmen urging on the men in dark blue, was quite something to see and hear.

John Charles (seen here in 1955 jousting with Jackie Henderson) was Wales' greatest-ever player. When this photo was taken he had just been transferred from Leeds United to Juventus for a British record fee of £65,000. He was one of the biggest football stars in the world.

But no stadium he ever played in was like the Scottish national stadium.

■ **Team v Wales, November 9th, 1955:**
1. **Tommy Younger (Hibernian)**
2. **Alex Parker (Falkirk)**
3. **Joe McDonald (Sunderland)**
4. **Bobby Evans (Celtic)**
5. **George Young, captain (Rangers)**
6. **Doug Cowie (Dundee)**
7. **Gordon Smith (Hibernian)**
8. **Bobby Johnstone (Manchester City)**
9. **Lawrie Reilly (Hibernian)**
10. **Bobby Collins (Hibernian)**
11. **Jackie Henderson (Portsmouth)**

■ England's players watch yet another
Hungary goal go in at Wembley, 1953.

A wake-up call

ENGLAND played Hungary in 1953 and were thrashed 6-3. Their first home defeat to a team from outside the British Isles was a huge shock to them. And those of us north of the Border were just as surprised at the quality of Magyar football.

The Hungarians visited Hampden the year after they'd been to Wembley. While the Scots did a little bit better, losing only 4-2, it was again clear the Hungarians were playing the game a lot better than we were.

Until these games, Continental football had been regarded as tippy-tappy nonsense by just about everyone caught up in the thud and blunder of British football. Insular know-it-alls, on both sides of the Border, thought there was little that we, who invented the game and had been playing it a lot longer, could learn from these people.

But these foreigners had been thinking about the game, and about tactics and formations, how to win possession, how to plan attacks, how to defend in a co-ordinated way. They had worked to become better at football while we had just played it. They put the emphasis on brain while we were still applying brawn.

This took a long time to sink in. For years afterwards British "experts" would still tell you the foreigners looked good with those one-twos, and triangles, but they couldn't shoot, couldn't head the ball properly. And they certainly didn't like a tackle.

But the results were undeniable.

The growth of TV games from World Cups, and teams visiting for competitive games in the new European tournaments, not just friendlies, cast yet more light into the dawning realisation that everyone else had overtaken us.

■ **Scotland played the Magyars at Hampden in unusual white-sleeved shirts, and put out a team without a Rangers or Celtic player for the first time since 1907.**

■ **Team v Hungary, December 8th, 1954:**
1. Fred Martin (Aberdeen)
2. Willie Cunningham, captain (Preston North End)
3. Harry Haddock (Clyde)
4. Tommy Docherty (Preston North End)
5. Jimmy Davidson (Partick Thistle)
6. John Cumming (Hearts)
7. Johnny McKenzie (Partick Thistle)
8. Bobby Johnstone (Hibernian)
9. Lawrie Reilly (Hibernian)
10. Jimmy Wardhaugh (Hearts)
11. Tommy Ring (Clyde)

World Cup Switzerland 1954

WE didn't win it. And we took a beating on the world stage – at the hands of Uruguay – that, even today, is talked of in hushed, shamed tones.

The whole cup trip was a shambles.

Rangers had arranged a tour of north America, so wouldn't allow any of their players to go to Switzerland. Celtic allowed three players to travel, but as we had strong sides like Hibs, Hearts, and Aberdeen (all of those clubs won the league in the 1950s) things didn't look so bad. We had good players. The part-time manager (who had to work with the team the SFA selection committee told him was going to play) was the respected Andy Beattie, who was doing very well with Huddersfield Town.

However, the SFA did their best to make life as difficult as possible for Andy and the team. After selecting a 22-man squad, then taking 18 players on a Scandinavian warm-up tour, they decreed that, due to their strict budget, just 13 players were to travel for the tournament itself. The full seven-man SFA selection committee went to Lucerne, though.

We were so disorganised that when the Austrians presented us with a pennant at the coin-toss before the first game, we didn't have one to give back.

Beattie resigned and flew home after the 1-0 defeat, saying it was impossible to work under such strictures. He couldn't change the team he'd been told to play.

The selection committee, stubborn to the last, accepted his resignation (thanks Andy, cheerio) and picked an unchanged team for the Uruguay game. The subsequent 7-0 thrashing at the hands of the reigning world champions was a severe blow to national pride.

Our players weren't ready for the the way the South Americans played football. We'd never seen anything like it. As *The Sunday Post's* respected correspondent, and former international, Jack Harkness said, "Those Uruguayans just wouldn't give us the ball to play with."

The thrashing wasn't a freak result, it was a fair reflection of the game. There were no quibbles about bad sportsmanship, play-acting, or biased refereeing. The Uruguayans cut us apart. Our forwards hardly touched the ball as it rarely got that far up the pitch.

Uruguay kept the ball, passing it between themselves again and again, and refused to stick to a 2-3-5 formation that our players were familiar with and so might know who they were supposed to be marking.

It didn't help that Scotland's players were wearing heavy woollen jerseys, no one having checked what summer temperatures might be in Switzerland. It turned out all those chocolate box photos of snow-topped mountains had been a cunning trick, and prepared us not at all for the heavy heat of a continental summer.

The tournament itself had a very odd format. The 16 nations were put into four groups, with two seeded and two unseeded teams. Both seeds played the non-seeds, but there was no seed v seed, or non-seed v non-seed games. So Scotland didn't play Czechoslovakia, despite being in the same group.

England had also qualified, and made it through to the first knock-out stage where Uruguay also showed them how the game should be played with a 4-2 beating that could easily have been more.

The tournament had started with a row over substitutes. The South American nations arrived in Zurich and declared that they wanted to use subs, despite a rule on no subs having been agreed months previously. Scotland's officials threatened to take the team home if the substitutes rules were altered in any way.

If only they had!

Indeed all the home nations were dead set against the idea of injured players, even goalkeepers, being replaced.

The next row was over, of all things, coin tosses. Refs at this World Cup insisted, "You are heads, you are tails" to team captains, not allowing them to choose. Jolly unsporting, moaned the SFA. This was surely one of the main reasons behind our poor performance!

And for the first time squad numbers were allocated that would remain for the duration of the tournament. Willie Ormond got unlucky shirt No. 13.

At the end of the tournament the Scots were offered a choice over how they would be paid. They could have a £15 appearance fee for each game (if they had played) – or could keep the thick winter shirts they'd played in.

■ **Team v Austria, June 16, 1954, at the Sportsplatz Hardturm, Zurich:**
1. Fred Martin (Aberdeen)
2. Willie Cunningham, captain (Preston North End)
3. John Aird (Burnley)
4. Tommy Docherty (Preston North End)
5. Jim Davidson (Partick Thistle)
6. Doug Cowie (Dundee)
7. John MacKenzie (Partick Thistle)
8. Willie Fernie (Celtic)
9. Neil Mochan (Celtic)
10. Allan Brown (Blackpool)
11. Willie Ormond (Hibernian)

■ **Team v Uruguay, June 19, 1954, at the Sankt Jakob Stadion, Basle:**
1. Fred Martin (Aberdeen)
2. Willie Cunningham, captain (Preston North End)
3. John Aird (Burnley)
4. Tommy Docherty (Preston North End)
5. Jim Davidson (Partick Thistle)
6. Doug Cowie (Dundee)
7. John MacKenzie (Partick Thistle)
8. Willie Fernie (Celtic)
9. Neil Mochan (Celtic)
10. Allan Brown (Blackpool)
11. Willie Ormond (Hibernian)

Bobby Evans (Celtic) and Bobby Johnstone (Hibs) also travelled, although Johnstone sustained an injury in training and returned home. He was replaced by George Hamilton (Aberdeen).

None of the three played a game.

■ Team v West Germany, May 22nd, 1957:
1. Tommy Younger (Liverpool)
2. Eric Caldow (Rangers)
3. John Hewie (Charlton Athletic)
4. Ian McColl (Rangers)
5. Bobby Evans (Celtic)
6. Tommy Docherty, captain (Preston NE)
7. Alex Scott (Rangers)
8. Bobby Collins (Celtic)
9. Jackie Mudie (Blackpool)
10. Sammy Baird (Rangers)
11. Tommy Ring (Clyde)

■ Despite what was said on the previous page, Scotland were still capable of pulling off momentous results from time to time. Above: Jackie Mudie (right) scores as Scotland beat World Cup holders West Germany 3-1 in Stuttgart in 1957.

■ In 1960 we went to Hungary and fought out a 3-3 draw. Though to be fair, the great Hungarian team of the mid-1950s had been broken up by then in the political upheaval of the 1956 Hungarian Revolution. The Soviets saw the pride the people had in their football team as anti-communist nationalism.

■ Team v Hungary, June 5th, 1960:
1. Bill Brown (Tottenham Hotspur)
2. Duncan MacKay (Celtic)
3. Eric Caldow (Rangers)
4. John Cumming (Hearts)
5. Bobby Evans, captain (Chelsea)
6. Dave Mackay (Tottenham Hotspur)
7. Graham Leggatt (Fulham)
8. George Herd (Clyde)
9. Alex Young (Hearts)
10. Willie Hunter (Motherwell)
11. Andy Weir (Motherwell)

ALMOST as bad as 1961 (see page 90) Scotland took a 7-2 thrashing at Wembley in 1955.

This was one of the best games 40-year-old Stanley Matthews ever played for his country. England's tactic on the day was simply to give the ball to Stan.

It is also testament to how different the game was back then when seeing the widespread praise Scotland's left-back, Harry Haddock, was given for "not resorting to the rough stuff" to stop Matthews.

■ **Left: Willie Cunningham and Billy Wright lead out the teams.**

■ **Right: Dennis Wilshaw scores England's first in the first minute despite the efforts of Cunningham on the line.**

■ **Team v England, April 2nd, 1955:**
1. **Fred Martin (Aberdeen)**
2. **Willie Cunningham, captain (Preston North End)**
3. **Harry Haddock (Clyde)**
4. **Tommy Docherty (Preston North End)**
5. **Jimmy Davidson (Partick Thistle)**
6. **John Cumming (Hearts)**
7. **John MacKenzie (Partick Thistle)**
8. **Bobby Johnstone (Manchester City)**
9. **Lawrie Reilly (Hibernian)**
10. **John McMillan (Airdrieonians)**
11. **Tommy Ring (Clyde)**

54

■ Lawrie Reilly is just beaten to the ball by keeper Harry Gregg in the Scotland-Northern Ireland Home International of 1956. It was the 36th of his 38 caps, a Scots record for a forward at the time. With 22 goals, he remains the fourth highest all-time Scottish international scorer. He scored six goals against England at Wembley in six games over the course of 12 years.

SCOTLAND'S next visit to Wembley, in 1957, was a little bit better. Tommy Ring gave us a lead in the first minute, but goals from West Brom's Derek Kevan and 20-year-old Manchester United starlet Duncan Edwards ruined what had looked like being a good day.

Scotland's international history is, of course, also a record of the teams – and remarkable players – we lined up against.

Throughout this book are references to the most famous names ever to play the game – Matthews, Pele, Best, Beckenbauer, Eusebio, Charles, Muller, Moore, Charlton, Panenka, Di Stefano, Fontaine, and many more. They all played against Scotland.

This page shows a player who might have taken his place among the best, Duncan Edwards, whose life was lost in the Munich Air Disaster 10 months later.

■ **Left: Almost on the goal line, 20-year-old Edwards clears what had looked a certain goal for Lawrie Reilly.**

■ **Team v England, April 6th, 1957:**
1. Tommy Younger (Liverpool)
2. Eric Caldow (Rangers)
3. John Hewie (Charlton Athletic)
4. Ian McColl (Rangers)
5. George Young, captain (Rangers)
6. Tommy Docherty (Preston North End)
7. Bobby Collins (Celtic)
8. Willie Fernie (Celtic)
9. Lawrie Reilly (Hibernian)
10. Jackie Mudie (Blackpool)
11. Tommy Ring (Clyde)

SCOTLAND'S three-nation World Cup 1958 qualifying group also contained Spain and Switzerland.

We beat the Spanish at Hampden, they beat us in Madrid. But the Spanish and Swiss fought out a 2-2 draw in their opening match. Our subsequent 2-1 win (Mudie and Collins) in Basel was the crucial result, leaving us knowing that another win against the Swiss at home would see us through.

It was a 2.30pm kick-off on a Wednesday afternoon, which explains the relatively low attendance of 58,811.

The Swiss treated the crowd to something they'd never seen before: a half-hour on-pitch warm-up that included stretches, passing to each other, and shooting practice. We assured each other that this sort of foreign trickery would never catch on.

Scotland won 3-2 with goals from Blackpool's Dundee-born centre-forward John (always known as Jackie) Mudie, Rangers winger Alex Scott, and Clyde inside-forward Archie Robertson.

Archie would, 20 years later, become Ally McCoist's science teacher at Hunter High School, East Kilbride. He also took the school's football team and Ally has always cited him as a great influence on his early career.

■ **Team v Switzerland, November 6th, 1957:**
1. Tommy Younger (Liverpool)
2. Alex Parker (Falkirk)
3. Alex Caldow (Rangers)
4. Willie Fernie (Celtic)
5. Bobby Evans (Celtic)
6. Tommy Docherty, captain (Preston North End)
7. Alex Scott (Rangers)
8. Bobby Collins (Celtic)
9. Jackie Mudie (Blackpool)
10. Archie Robertson (Clyde)
11. Tommy Ring (Clyde)

■ **Robertson, half hidden by Swiss keeper Eugene Parlier, gets Scotland's first goal on 27 minutes. Sweden, here we come!**

World Cup Sweden 1958

WE didn't win it. Though we did better than we had four years previously – albeit only slightly better.

This remains the only World Cup finals tournament for which all of the four UK home nations qualified.

There were 16 teams competing, starting in groups of four. But this time every country played all of the others in the group. We were in Group 2, with France, Yugoslavia, and Paraguay.

We managed to take 22 players to this tournament, though line-ups were still picked by the selection committee. The manager had a say (or would have done if we'd had a manager) and then coached the players.

The boss should have been Matt Busby on a part-time basis alongside his job at Manchester United. But Busby was badly injured in the Munich Air Disaster so Dawson Walker, Clyde FC's trainer, took on the manager role on a temporary basis.

Walker had never played the game at professional level and was a fitness and massage man rather than a football tactician. He did what he could, and no fault for what happened should be attached to a man put in a very difficult position.

Our first game was against Yugoslavia and we got a creditable 1-1 draw against a team that had thumped England 5-0 in a warm-up game just a few weeks previously.

That was our highlight of the tournament.

The big mistake was the Paraguay match. The Scotland selectors sent players Tommy Docherty and Archie Robertson to watch the Paraguayans' first game. Docherty appeared to have been dropped from the team to play Yugoslavia for the crime of disagreeing with SFA chairman George Graham on a football matter.

In any case, the two spies reported that the South Americans were hard as nails, but no great shakes as footballers, as they lost heavily, 7-3, to France.

The Scots selectors, instead of playing the more robust Dave Mackay and Sammy Baird, picked the diminutive though highly-skilled Willie Fernie and Archie Robertson.

They thought our ball players would dance past the tough guys, but dancing is difficult when someone is trying to make mashed potato of your knees.

We lost 3-2.

By the time of the third match, we knew qualification was unlikely. We had to beat France by a large margin and hope Paraguay would beat the Yugoslavs, but by not such a large margin.

France announced they were dropping keeper Francois Remetter for shouting at the rest of his team too much during their previous two games. His place was taken by Claude Abbes.

Just Fontaine, on his way to the all-time Finals goal-scoring record of 13, and Raymond Kopa, had the French two up by half-time. Sammy Baird put one past the (presumably suitably quiet) Abbes midway through the second half, but we were on our way home having gathered just one point.

There was a storm of criticism waiting for the SFA.

The decision to go to Sweden without a manager was lambasted. All football teams have a manager. The Munich tragedy that denied Scotland the services of Busby was a clear four months before the tournament.

No one was in charge of the team. The players were handed the committee's chosen line-up on a sheet of paper and had to make up their own minds how they'd play, what the dangers of the opposition might be, and give each other motivational or tactical talks.

Indeed, the whole concept of having SFA committee members – club chairmen and secretaries, most of whom were businessmen who had never played the game professionally – retiring in secret to pick the team was decmed ludicrous and old fashioned.

Even after being put out of the tournament, no SFA official stayed on in Sweden to learn how other, more successful, nations organised themselves for a World Cup.

The set-up was decried as "amateurish" and "the laughing stock of world football". We vowed that, next time, it would all be different.

The problem was that "next time" was a long time coming.

■ **Team v Yugoslavia, June 8th, 1958, at the Arsovallen Stadium, Vasteras:**
1. Tommy Younger, captain (Liverpool)
2. Eric Caldow (Rangers)
3. John Hewie (Charlton Athletic)
4. Eddie Turnbull (Hibernian)
5. Bobby Evans (Celtic)
6. Doug Cowie (Dundee)
7. Graham Leggat (Aberdeen)
8. Jimmy Murray (Hearts)
9. Jackie Mudie (Blackpool)
10. Bobby Collins (Celtic)
11. Stewart Imlach (Nottingham Forest)

■ **Team v Paraguay, June 11th, 1958, at the Idrottsparken, Norrkoping:**
1. Tommy Younger, captain (Liverpool)
2. Alex Parker (Everton)
3. Eric Caldow (Rangers)
4. Eddie Turnbull (Hibernian)
5. Bobby Evans (Celtic)
6. Doug Cowie (Dundee)
7. Graham Leggat (Aberdeen)
8. Bobby Collins (Celtic)
9. Jackie Mudie (Blackpool)
10. Archie Robertson (Clyde)
11. Willie Fernie (Celtic)

■ **Team v France, June 15th, 1958, at the Eyravallen, Orebro:**
1. Bill Brown (Dundee)
2. Eric Caldow (Rangers)
3. John Hewie (Charlton Athletic)
4. Eddie Turnbull (Hibernian)
5. Bobby Evans, captain (Celtic)
6. Dave Mackay (Hearts)
7. Bobby Collins (Celtic)
8. Jimmy Murray (Hearts)
9. Jackie Mudie (Blackpool)
10. Sammy Baird (Rangers)
11. Stewart Imlach (Nottingham Forest)

To wear the shirt

THERE have been many styles of Scotland strip over the years. Each supporter has his or her favourite, which is often nothing to do with design and everything to do with the fond memories they hold of when they were younger and the good times they enjoyed watching a team play in that shirt.

But for the players, the shirt is a thing of magical properties.

There is a healthy online trade in match-worn shirts in the football world these days. Punters seem to like purchasing a shirt worn by their heroes in an actual game. Club strips are fairly common. But finding international shirts for sale is a rare thing.

Players don't lightly give away their international shirts.

Pulling on the colours of your country is a significant moment in any player's life. If you read their autobiographies, a high proportion describe feelings of reverence the first time they saw their national shirt hanging on a peg waiting for them.

And those shirts are among the most valued heirlooms a player has. They often present their international shirts to their families and these shirts will, in turn, be passed down to children and grandchildren.

Every Scotland shirt you see on the back of a player shown on these pages is now probably a treasured item kept in the safest of safe places by a proud Scottish family. In the photos they look fresh and pristine, but nowadays will be old and probably delicate items. They are the physical embodiment of a man's life, and his greatest achievements.

■ **Left: Alex Scott (Scotland 1956-66).**
■ **Right: John Hewie (Scotland 1956-60).**

■ 1951. Scotland, playing with 10 home-based men, went to Wembley and beat the English – Matthews, Finney, the lot of them – 3-2.

■ Team v England, April 14th, 1951:
1. Jimmy Cowan (Morton)
2. George Young, captain (Rangers)
3. Sammy Cox (Rangers)
4. Bobby Evans (Celtic)
5. Willie Woodburn (Rangers)
6. Willie Redpath (Motherwell)
7. Willie Waddell (Rangers)
8. Bobby Johnstone (Hibernian)
9. Lawrie Reilly (Hibernian)
10. Billy Steel (Dundee)
11. Billy Liddell (Liverpool)

They always gave a good pep talk

THIS book doesn't intend to throw many thanks the way of the English, but there is one enduring piece of help that they almost always give the Scottish team that deserves recognition.

The arrogance, short memories, and sheer ignorance of their newspaper columnists and TV and radio commentators provides excellent pep talks.

Since the very first international in 1872, the English have written off the Scots' chances. According to their wise media men, every time a dark blue XI has come up against a white-shirted team, the Scots will be lucky to get out of their own half, certainly won't score a goal, and shouldn't really be on the same pitch as the supermen of the south.

They often don't even know the names of our home-based players.

George Young played in many a Scotland game. His favourite, however (as revealed in his 1957 autobiography *George Young Talks Football*) was the England-Scotland encounter at Wembley in April 1949. It turned out to be Scotland's first Home International Championship win since the war.

The reason George enjoyed the game so much was because the newspapers that he and the rest of the team had read over breakfast didn't harbour even an inkling that England might lose.

They drooled over the names in their own side: the Blackpool duo Stan Mortensen and Stanley Matthews, Newcastle icon Jackie Milburn, Wolves superstar Billy Wright, Preston North End's all-time-greatest player Tom Finney, and Stoke centre-half Neil Franklin – who was an excellent player but one the English have airbrushed out of history as he later walked out on the national side for a lucrative contract in Colombia.

The sages of the London Press didn't give one man in the Scots team a mention.

In the game, however, powerful George, the steely Willie Woodburn, hard-running Willie Waddell, deadly Lawrie Reilly, and the wide, bustling shoulders of Billy Houliston swarmed all over the English and won 3-1.

I hasten to add, it isn't usually the English players who are guilty.

There often seems to be mutual respect and even friendship between those who play the game. It is the chattering classes who do the damage.

Amazingly, they've been doing this for a century and a half, and will probably keep on doing it for another century and a half.

Long may it continue. We in Scotland would like to offer our heartfelt thanks for the all the inspirational and motivational work.

SCOTLAND versus Wales in November 1959. It was a 1-1 draw, with Graham Leggat getting Scotland's goal in the 46th minute.

The British Home Championship was shared that season, with Scotland, England and Wales all finishing on four points. Scotland had the superior goal average, but that didn't count.

The SFA were roundly criticised after this game for sending out ball boys in red tops of exactly the same shade as the Welsh team.

■ **Right: An Ian St John header goes just over the bar. The Saint is lying beside Welsh keeper Alf Kelsey.**

■ **Team v Wales, November 4th, 1959:**
1. **Bill Brown (Tottenham Hotspur)**
2. **Eric Caldow (Rangers)**
3. **John Hewie (Charlton Athletic)**
4. **Dave Mackay (Tottenham Hotspur)**
5. **Bobby Evans, captain (Celtic)**
6. **Bert McCann (Motherwell)**
7. **Graham Leggat (Fulham)**
8. **John White (Tottenham)**
9. **Ian St John (Motherwell)**
10. **Denis Law (Huddersfield Town)**
11. **Bertie Auld (Celtic)**

Scotland's unique problem

THE 1950s drew to a close with Scotland, not for the first, or last, time guilty of underperforming. The last Auld Enemy game of the decade was a 1-0 loss at Wembley to a Bobby Charlton header.

Again not for the first or last time, post-match arguments among fans and newspaper reporters alike, were over whether players who were stars in the English leagues were any better than those playing their football in Scotland.

This was the game in which England skipper Billy Wright became the first man in world football to win 100 caps for his country. He was carried off the Wembley pitch on the shoulders of his teammates, with the Scotland players sportingly applauding and clapping him on the back on the way.

This was the closest our forward line got to a man who, to be fair, was a gifted centre-half, all afternoon.

Scotland that day included centre-forward John Dick making his first and last appearance in dark blue. A Scottish selector had taken in a West Ham United match in which the tall and powerful Dick scored a couple of goals and played well. The following week, the Govan laddie was named in the Scotland team.

Other one-cap-wonders in this era included Bolton's Aberdeen-born inside-forward Willie Moir, Arsenal's Edinburgh-born inside-forward Jimmy Logie, and Southampton's goalkeeper Ian Black, another Aberdeen loon.

These men weren't bad players by any means, but these one-time-only glimpses of Anglos in Scotland strips fuelled the fires of debate over whether a man plying his trade in the supposedly superior English First Division was any better than a player banging in goals at Ibrox, Celtic Park, Tynecastle, Pittodrie, and Easter Road.

These weren't new issues back then – and have never gone away since.

Nowadays, arguments rage in places like Brazil and Argentina (and many other nations) over whether stars playing far away in Europe's highly-paid leagues are better than those still at home.

But this is a fairly modern debate in these countries, it has been raging in Scotland for 150 years.

Scotland was, for decades, unique in world football in having so many players who were playing with clubs not in their home country.

It's an argument which we have never resolved.

■ Right: Bobby Evans and Billy Wright lead out the teams for the 1959 England-Scotland game.

■ Two more shots from the 1959 England-Scotland clash at Wembley. Left: Celtic's Duncan MacKay gets in a tackle on England's Bolton Wanderers winger Doug Holden. Holden remains the last player alive who played in the famous 1953 "Matthews" FA Cup Final.

■ Right: Prime Minister Harold Macmillan shakes the hand of John Dick. The West Ham striker, lined up beside future Scotland manager Tommy Docherty, was about to make his one and only Scotland appearance. John played 364 games for West Ham, and remains third on the East London club's all-time top-scorer list with 176 goals.

■ Team v England, April 11th, 1959:
1. Bill Brown (Dundee)
2. Duncan MacKay (Celtic)
3. Eric Caldow (Rangers)
4. Tommy Docherty (Arsenal)
5. Bobby Evans, captain (Celtic)
6. Dave Mackay (Tottenham Hotspur)
7. Graham Leggat (Fulham)
8. Bobby Collins (Everton)
9. David Herd (Arsenal)
10. John Dick (West Ham United)
11. Willie Ormond (Hibernian)

■ **More action from Wembley 1959. A young Bobby Charlton, aged 21 at the time, gets the only goal of the game in the second half, with what was, you'd have to admit, a good leap and downward header.**

■ **Scotland might have scored after English keeper Eddie Hopkinson fumbled a Tommy Docherty cross. David Herd got a foot to the ball and his prod goalwards was going in until it hit his fellow striker Graham Leggat on the bahookie. Such tales of bizarre bad luck are common in Scotland's international football history.**

We had the

COMPARING strikers of one era with those of another era is almost always a futile exercise.

The style of football will be different, the opponents are different, the pitches are different. There are too many variables to really make any sense of a today/yesterday comparison.

However, one aspect of Scottish international players of the third decade of the 21st Century, and the 1950s, '60s and '70s does merit remark.

Scotland's strikers back in those days, if Denis Law and Ian St John are taken as examples, were the main men for Manchester United and Liverpool, arguably the two foremost football clubs in

■ **Denis Law of Manchester United.**

very best

England, and among the biggest and richest clubs in the world.

That isn't the case today.

All of football has changed. It is now truly a global game. Club recruitment is done on a worldwide scale.

It is naive to suggest all the biggest clubs in the world should take their strikers from a wee country off the coast of northern Europe.

Perhaps, though, it could be said that Scottish supporters walked taller, held their heads higher, when it was openly acknowledged that the greatest, most expensive footballers were grown in our country.

Back then, it seemed natural.

We all knew, and the clubs knew, that Scottish players were the best in the world.

■ **Ian St John, of Liverpool.**

The Wizards

THE Wembley Wizards of 1928 had a reunion at Glasgow's Central Hotel in April 1958 to mark 30 years since one of the greatest performances in Scottish football history.

The "joke starter" on the menu was Grilled Sassenachs on Toast.

Sportingly, legendary Everton forward Dixie Dean, who had been in the England team that day, also attended the dinner though he declined to be in this photo.

What a team the Wizards were. They trounced England 5-1 with a display of running and quick passing that mesmerised, and ruthlessly cut through, the English defence.

The line up at the dinner (right) is, from left:

Jimmy Kerr (trainer),
Tully Craig (reserve),
Jimmy Gibson,
Tommy Law,
Tommy (Tiny) Bradshaw,
Jack Harkness,
Jimmy Dunn,
Alan Morton,
Jimmy Nelson,
Jimmy McMullan,
Willie Bell, the referee.

■ **Team v England, March 31st, 1928:**
1. **Jack Harkness (Queen's Park)**
2. **Jimmy Nelson (Cardiff City)**
3. **Tommy Law (Chelsea)**
4. **Jimmy Gibson (Aston Villa)**
5. **Tommy Bradshaw (Bury)**
6. **Jimmy McMullan, captain (Man. City)**
7. **Alex Jackson (Huddersfield Town)**
8. **Jimmy Dunn (Hibernian)**
9. **Hughie Gallacher (Newcastle United)**
10. **Alex James (Preston North End)**
11. **Alan Morton (Rangers)**

Hughie Gallacher had tragically died the previous year (see next page). Alex James died of cancer in 1953, aged 51. Alex Jackson was killed in a traffic accident while serving with the Army in Egypt in 1946, aged 41.

78

The wizard in chief, Hughie Gallacher

SCOTLAND has never seen the likes of Hughie Gallacher kick a ba' again, though almost a century of football has passed since he was in his prime. He was the greatest centre-forward that the world has ever seen.

Hugh Kilpatrick Gallacher was born in Bellshill in 1903 and worked down the pit when he was 15.

Though not a tall man at 5 feet 5 inches, he was a giant on a football field. His meteoric rise in the professional game began at the newly-formed Queen of the South, a non-league team, in 1921.

He then spent four years at Airdrieonians, scoring 100 goals in 129 games and winning the 1924 Scottish Cup. Airdrie had never won a major trophy before, and have never won one since.

Despite threats that the Broomfield stand would be burned down, Hughie was given a sensational transfer to Newcastle United in 1925.

He remains the most prolific striker in Newcastle's history, scoring 143 goals in 174 games. He was bought by big-spending Chelsea in 1930, where he scored 81 goals in 144 games.

As a Scotland player, Gallacher's record is remarkable.

In an era of significantly fewer international matches, Hughie scored 23 goals in 20 games, third on the all-time list. He got a further six goals in two Scottish League appearances while at Airdrie.

He was a leader on the field. Every game revolved around him. Every time this charismatic, lightning-fast, highly-skilled superstar got on the ball it looked like something would happen. Big, powerful, evil-intentioned centre-halves would attempt to cut him down, but Hughie, never a shrinking violet, often got his retribution in first. Off-the-ball incidents weren't unusual around him.

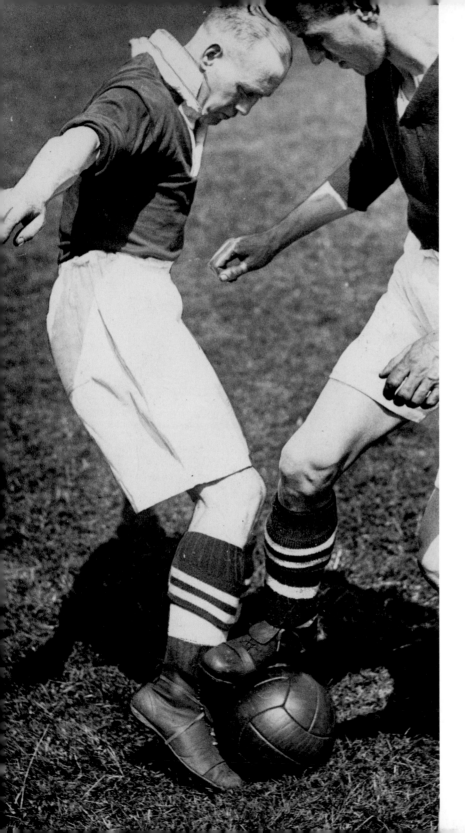

WHAT would Hughie be worth in the transfer market of today? It's a good question.

To modern eyes, his style could perhaps best be compared to Diego Maradona, with touches of Lionel Messi thrown in. But Hughie was much more of a two-footed player than the pronounced "leftie" Maradona.

The Messi comparison is valid because of his dribbling skills, the ability to go past a man as if he was a wooden post. But Gallacher was a more robust player than the modern Argentinian striker. Hughie had to be a 1920s-era centre-forward who went up for high balls against defenders a foot taller than he was.

His timing in the air was magnificent. His ability to generate power with his neck muscles could be compared to Denis Law.

Hughie could shield a ball like Kenny Dalglish, shoot like Peter Lorimer, and led his team by sheer force of will like Billy Bremner or Graeme Souness.

The game has changed greatly since the 1920s, of course, but rest assured that Hughie would be a star in the modern game. Skill, a good first touch, the eye-to-foot coordination required to strike a ball cleanly, as well as the footballing intelligence needed to be in the right place at just the right time – these things have not changed.

The things Hughie did with a ball, the iron will to win that made him such a fierce competitor, the leadership qualities, the natural footballing abilities, would all still be highly prized today.

Hughie was a phenomenon. A one-off footballer who would have thrived in any era. With modern training, a scientifically-defined diet, and the many other benefits of advanced sports science, he'd be a global superstar today.

■ March 25th, 1933. Hughie makes his point vehemently after referee G.C. Denton ruled out a Chelsea "goal" against West Brom.

■ The Black Country side won 2-1, though Hughie got the Chelsea goal. Of course.

THERE is a long tradition, almost an expectation, that great footballers are troubled footballers. And so it was with Hughie.

He was good, and he knew it. He liked a party, and had been accused of being drunk while playing. He was always a volatile man and put in a few tackles – and punches – that might have brought the game into disrepute (as they used to say at the time).

Hughie was loved by the Geordies who stood on the terraces to sing his name, but often at loggerheads with the Newcastle United directors.

But he was made club captain, and in the 1926-27 season scored 36 goals in 38 league games, still a record at St James' Park.

■ **Right: Photos that haven't been seen for 70 years – Hughie with his cherished second wife Hannah.**

She was the daughter of the landlord of Hughie's favourite Newcastle pub and just 17 when they met. Hughie had been married to Annie when he was himself 17 in Bellshill, but the marriage had long since broken down. Annie was in Scotland with their son Jackie, who would go on to become a prolific striker with Celtic.

But Hannah's family were unhappy at the prospect of their respectable daughter "going around with a married man" and several times hunted down Hughie to threaten him with violence.

Hughie sought a divorce from his first wife, but this was difficult and expensive in those days and money problems were said to be at the root of the Newcastle directors' decision to sell him to Chelsea in 1930.

The supporters were aghast, just as the Airdrie fans had been when he had first moved to England.

He married Hannah, but was declared bankrupt in 1934. A transfer to Derby County followed, though allegations of financial irregularities over a signing-on fee would surface. The Derby manager George Jobey was banned from the game sine die, though no action was taken against Hughie.

He moved on to Notts County, then Grimsby, scoring goals all the way, before in 1938 finally returning to Gateshead on his beloved Tyneside where he would end his career. And his life.

■ **Left: Hughie lines up in a Chelsea strip for the first time.**

■ **Right: After his playing career ended with the suspension of all football at the outbreak of the second world war, Hughie worked with a Gateshead mining engineering company.**

Hughie's beloved Hannah died on December 31st, 1950. She had been ill for a while with a heart condition. Hughie was left with their three sons to look after.

By the summer of 1957 the two elder boys had left home to serve with the RAF. One night, the always-quick-to-anger Hughie threw a glass ashtray towards his son Mattie. It cut his head. The police were called to the rumpus and to his horror Hughie was charged with assaulting his son, who was taken into care.

Hughie was a proud man and devoted to his boys. The looming court case played heavily on his mind.

The newspapers and street gossips scourged him. The fallen star was hounded with unfounded allegations of abuse and neglect.

In the lead-up to the court date Hughie took to roaming the streets. He drank too much and didn't talk enough. Those who saw him described the formerly cocky, devil-may-care superstar as a broken man.

Hughie told one journalist friend: "It's no use fighting this when you know you can't win. My life is finished. Drink has been my downfall. If I could have kept off the drink I would have been a different man."

The hearing was set for Wednesday, June 12th, 1957. On the night before, the 11th, two young lads were looking out for locomotive numbers from a bridge over the railway at Low Fell, a suburb of Gateshead and not far from Hughie's home on The Avenue, Sheriff Hill. The trainspotting boys saw a disconsolate figure, a lonely man walking up and down close to the track.

As the York-Edinburgh express came through,

Hughie stepped in front of the train. His battered and headless body was found 100 yards down the line.

Hughie was 54.

The obituaries were fulsome in their praise. "Hughie of the magic feet is dead" said one headline.

His funeral was supposed to be a private affair, but friends and former players lined the route to Newcastle Crematorium. The Toon turned out in droves to say farewell to their club's greatest hero.

■ Football nations of the world recognise the player-in-a-hundred-years phenomenon. A player born among them who might be described as the best on the planet in his time. A player who wins games on his own.

Bigger countries see more candidates. Pele could be joined by Ronaldo Nazario and Ronaldinho in Brazil. Maradona was followed by Messi in Argentina. France might have to choose between Platini and Zidane. Smaller countries have had the likes of Cruyff (Holland), Puskas (Hungary), Stoichkov (Bulgaria), Best (Northern Ireland), Ibrahimovic (Sweden), and Ronaldo (Portugal).

England has had some very good players – Dean, Matthews, Charlton – but are perhaps still waiting for a true best-of-his-era star. Some great footballing nations haven't really had a serious candidate at all.

Scotland has had great players – McGrory, Law, Johnstone, Baxter, and Dalglish to name a few.

Above them all, though, we had Hughie Gallacher.

It is merely an accident of time that robs us of footage with which to show off our best-in-the-world genius.

■ Hughie, Hannah and two of their sons, Tommy and Hughie Junior, pictured in 1945.

The worst six minutes in history

SATURDAY the 15th of April, 1961, at the Empire Stadium, Wembley. Kick-off 3pm.

We'll have to talk about this, like it or not. No book that claims to show the Scottish international team's exploits from this era can ignore this game. We lost, and we lost badly, to our oldest and most bitter foes. It was 9-3. It still hurts, six decades later.

It has to be said that, perhaps surprisingly, for most of the game Scotland weren't that bad. This wasn't Scotland's worst-ever full game performance. It was Scotland's worst-ever six-minute performance.

The joke for many years was: "What time is it? It's nine past Haffey!" And the blame has been loaded on to the shoulders of goalkeeper Frank Haffey.

He was, it is true, an eccentric goalkeeper. This was a man who once attempted to take a quick goal kick for Celtic and sclaffed the ball into his own net. This was a man who once took a penalty for Celtic then stood to applaud the other goalkeeper's save rather than sprint back to his own box. And everyone who knew him said what a great singer he was.

But heaping all the problems on Frank Haffey was just an easy way to point to a scapegoat. Frank didn't have a good game, it is true. He was probably at fault for two of the goals.

But every man in the Scotland team had a bad game that day.

By contrast, England – who were in the middle of a rich vein of form – had one of those games where everything they tried came off, and (more importantly) went into the net. Jimmy Greaves, Bobby Charlton and Johnny Haynes were superb, almost unplayable the whole game. And for six minutes in the second half they were truly God-like.

Scotland, 3-0 down at half-time, came out all-guns-blazing after the break and had the score at 3-2 within eight minutes with goals from Dave Mackay and Davie Wilson. At that point we looked like we were about to pull off the greatest ever Scotland comeback.

England then scored another couple, but Pat Quinn got the margin back to two in the 75th minute. At this point, 5-3 down, it was a beating but not a humiliation.

But then, from the 80th to 85th minutes, the world turned upside down. In roughly six minutes of play, Scotland let in four goals. There had never been anything like it before, and there never has been since.

■ **Right: Frank Haffey sprawled on the turf, and Eric Caldow looking on with equal agony, as the seventh goes in.**

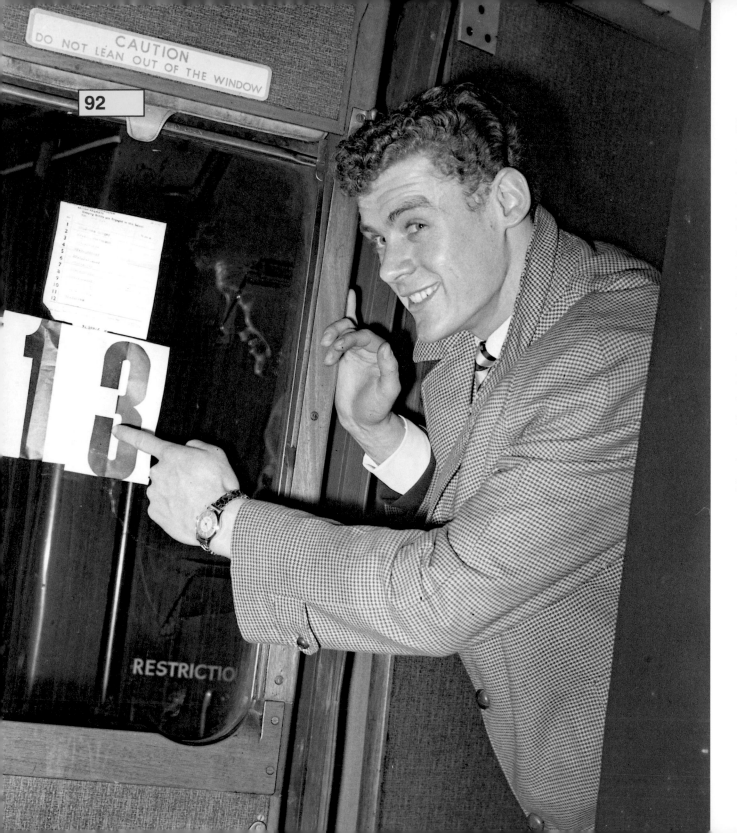

■ Ever quick with a joke, Frank Haffey had a laugh and posed for the photographers when it was discovered that he, and the rest of the Scotland-based players, were in "unlucky" carriage 13 for the rail journey from Glasgow to London for that 1961 game.

We needed all the luck we could get, Frank!

Scotland's 1961 team was fairly inexperienced.

Bobby Shearer, Billy McNeill, Johnny MacLeod and Pat Quinn all made their debuts in the game. It was just a second cap for Frank Haffey and a third for Davie Wilson.

Only Eric Caldow (28th cap) and Dave Mackay (15th cap) had previously played at Wembley. Denis Law (11th cap) was about to be transferred to Torino for £110,000 – a record fee in a deal involving a British player.

■ **Right: Captains Eric Caldow and Johnny Haynes lead out the teams.**

■ **Team v England, April 15th, 1961:**
1. **Frank Haffey (Celtic)**
2. **Bobby Shearer (Rangers)**
3. **Eric Caldow, captain (Rangers)**
4. **Dave Mackay (Tottenham Hotspur)**
5. **Billy McNeill (Celtic)**
6. **Bert McCann (Motherwell)**
7. **Johnny MacLeod (Hibernian)**
8. **Denis Law (Manchester City)**
9. **Ian St John (Motherwell)**
10. **Pat Quinn (Motherwell)**
11. **Davie Wilson (Rangers)**

■ Jimmy Greaves gets England's second, and (right) third goals. Chelsea star Greaves was also about to be transferred to Italy, but would be back in England, with Spurs, within six months.

Widely regarded as Fulham's greatest ever player – there is a statue of him outside Craven Cottage – Haynes moved to Scotland after his playing career and became a Hearts supporter.

His wife Avril, was Scottish, and she and Johnny ran a laundry business in Edinburgh for many years.

In a career of many fine performances, that day at Wembley in 1961 was among his best – though outside Fulham he was never feted quite so much as Greaves or Bobby Charlton.

■ **Johnny Haynes, on the right of this photo, gets England's 6th goal.**

■ **England's Bobby Smith puts the ninth past Frank Haffey. It was a horrible moment on a horrible day.**

Frank Haffey made 201 appearances for Celtic and won two Scotland caps (this game was his second). He was transferred to Swindon in 1963, but emigrated to Australia in 1965, where he still lives.

He became a singer on the Aussie cabaret circuit.

Everyone liked him. Any reference or reminiscence of him in his playing days, or later as a goalkeeping coach in Australia, tells of what a charismatic guy he is.

It should also be remembered that when he played for Scotland against England the previous year, Hampden 1960, he saved a Bobby Charlton penalty to secure a 1-1 draw.

He had one fairly bad game and by goalkeeping standards, when every mistake results in a goal, it wasn't even that bad a performance. Yet he carries the can. It is his name that is mentioned whenever that nine-goal rout at Wembley is remembered.

It is long past time that we forgave Frank Haffey. How about Frank Haffey for the Scottish Football Hall of Fame?

■ **Handshakes after the game. Haffey (far left) looks like a man alone with his thoughts.**

■ England's 8th, a hat-trick for Greaves.

What is always forgotten about 1961 is that, effectively, Scotland played with 10 men.

Motherwell left-half Bert McCann had a 12-hour nosebleed the day before the game. A surgeon eventually attempted a minor op to stem the flow at 11pm on the Friday night.

Bert didn't sleep due to the pain, another torturous 24 hours for him after the entire party having an uncomfortable, sleep-deprived journey the previous night on the overnght train from Glasgow.

At 8am on the Saturday he failed a fitness test, being unable to run even a short distance.

But the travelling reserve, Killie's Andy Kerr, was a centre-forward. Manager Ian McColl asked Bert to play. He heroically did his best in his weakened state but played the entire game in pain from the op, with blood still pouring from his nose.

■ **Left: Johnny Haynes receives the British International Championship Trophy from the Queen. This was the first time she'd ever been to a Scotland-England game.**

The 1960s. We had a team that could stand tall in world football. But didn't

IT isn't a wry joke, or said with a wink of the eye. It is true. Scotland, in the 1960s, had one of the best football teams in the world. We had a pool of players that was stuffed full of world-class talent. We could have, perhaps should have, won something.

We had Denis Law, Billy McNeill, John Greig, Jimmy Johnstone, Alan Gilzean, Jim Baxter, John White, Billy Bremner . . . and Frank Haffey.

The trouble was, they didn't always play up to the standard they could. Or, at least, didn't always play as a team in the way they might have done.

When the lads in the dark blue shirts got it right, it was wonderful. We gave Spain six at the Bernabeu, beat a Czechoslovakia team that was on its way to a World Cup Final – and, of course, became unofficial world champions ourselves.

We held a West German side containing Beckenbauer, Muller, Overath (and Bertie Vogts) to 1-1 in a World Cup Qualifier. We drew with the fabulous Brazil team that could boast all the tricks of Pele, Jairzinho, and Gerson. But then, we also shipped nine against England and suffered the worst-attended home game in Scottish international history.

Our club sides tore through Europe. Celtic won the European Cup and made it to several other semis, Rangers were in two Cup Winners' Cup Finals, and Kilmarnock, Dunfermline and Dundee contested semi-finals. We were among Europe's big football nations.

But we didn't qualify for the 1962, 1966, or 1970 World Cup Finals Tournaments.

You might argue the players were never together long enough to get to know each other, far less work on tactics and set-pieces. And there were always lots of call-offs. The 11 that beat England 3-2 at Wembley in 1967 never took to the field again as a team.

You might say we were unlucky. However it is described, we didn't do ourselves justice.

■ **Team v Northern Ireland, October 7th, 1961:**
1. **Bill Brown (Tottenham Hotspur)**
2. **Duncan MacKay (Celtic)**
3. **Eric Caldow, captain (Rangers)**
4. **Paddy Crerand (Celtic)**
5. **Billy McNeill (Celtic)**
6. **Jim Baxter (Rangers)**
7. **Alex Scott (Rangers)**
8. **John White (Tottenham Hotspur)**
9. **Ian St John (Liverpool)**
10. **Ralph Brand (Rangers)**
11. **Davie Wilson (Rangers)**

■ **Manchester United keeper Harry Gregg can only watch in despair as a smiling Alex Scott (right) scores Scotland's second against Northern Ireland at Windsor Park in a 6-1 victory.**

JOE BAKER was the unluckiest Scotsman who ever lived. Joe was Scottish. His mother was Scottish. His father, although born in Liverpool, raised his son in Scotland.

But Joe's father, a sailor, took the family to America then to England for a short stay in 1940 (during the war, you went where you were told), where Joe was born. But then they all moved permanently back north of the border.

Joe thought of himself as Scottish, talked with a Scots accent, and played football in Scotland. He was even selected for the Scottish Schoolboys team.

But, under the strict rules of the time, he was born in England so when it came to representing his country at full international level, it had to be England.

That was that, there was no wriggle-room. His birth certificate said England so he was English.

Joe was an accomplished centre-forward.

He scored 102 goals for Hibs, including an astonishing 42 in 33 games in the 1959-60 season. In 1961 he was sensationally transferred to Torino for £75,000 to play alongside Denis Law.

It's every laddie's dream to play in a Scotland-England game, and Joe achieved this in 1960 – although wearing a white shirt.

But he was carried off the Hampden pitch (left) after injuring his shoulder in the first half of the 1-1 draw when leaping a Frank Haffey dive at his feet.

■ **Team v England, April 9th, 1960:**
1. **Frank Haffey (Celtic)**
2. **Duncan MacKay (Celtic)**
3. **Eric Caldow (Rangers)**
4. **John Cumming (Hearts)**
5. **Bobby Evans, captain (Celtic)**
6. **Bert McCann (Motherwell)**
7. **Graham Leggat (Fulham)**
8. **Alex Young (Hearts)**
9. **Ian St John (Motherwell)**
10. **Denis Law (Manchester City)**
11. **Andy Weir (Motherwell)**

Almost winning the World Cup 1962

ONLY 57 nations entered the 1962 World Cup. Chile, were automatically in the finals as hosts, and defending champions Brazil had to be there. The other 14 nations were arrived at by a variety of strangely-organised qualifying groups.

African and Asian nations who won their groups had to play off against European or South American countries to get to Chile, but none did. Only Mexico, outside of the world's two football powerhouse continents, made it through. FIFA vowed that this would never happen again, although the African nations boycotted the 1966 World Cup in further protest.

Scotland's job in 1961, however, was simple – win a three-nation group, also containing Czechoslovakia and the Republic of Ireland, to get through.

It started well.

Our home-and-away double-header with the Irish saw a 4-1 win in Glasgow on May 3rd 1961, and a 3-0 victory in Dublin four days later.

Then, however, we were humbled 4-0 in Bratislava on May 14th.

But we got revenge the following September at Hampden in a game that was probably one of Scotland's best performances since the war, although the crowd was a lowly 56,000.

We were behind twice but Ian St John equalised the first time, then Denis Law got two late goals to record a famous 3-2 win.

So Czechoslovakia's task was to beat the Republic twice to match our points total. This they duly did, handsomely, 3-1 and 7-1.

These were the days before goal difference (or average) was taken into account, which was just as well as their plus-11 was much better than our plus-3. So we had to play off at a neutral venue, which was decided as the Heysel Stadium in Brussels.

Possibly because they were unused to playing under floodlights the Czechs (as it was acceptable to call them in those days) insisted on an afternoon kick off.

In front of a disappointing 7,000 crowd (and with a team weakened by injuries to Billy McNeill, Davie Wilson and Bill Brown) it was 2-2 at full-time, both of Scotland's goals scored by 23-year-old Ian St John.

We had been ahead twice and the second Cezch equaliser had looked more than a little iffy, a shot that hit the bar, then came down on the line.

But extra time it was, and the Czechs got another couple of goals and we were out.

Czechoslovakia made it to the final of World Cup 1962. They went a goal up after 15 minutes but lost 3-1 to Brazil. Scotland, in the same position, would surely have found an extra gear to win the thing!

■ One of the now sadly departed Ian St John's finest games in a Scotland shirt. The Saint's first goal in Brussels, with Czechoslovakia's Viliam Schrojf (half hidden by the post) displaying an unusual goalkeeping technique.

More action from the Brussels play-off game of 1961.

■ **Left: The Saint gets ready to challenge for a corner (though it looks like he is attempting to header one of the globes of the Brussels Atomium).**

■ **Right: Denis Law in typically combative pose, with keeper Schrojf again showing some unorthodox moves.**

■ Team v Czechoslovakia, November 29th, 1961:
1. Eddie Connachan (Dunfermline Athletic)
2. Alex Hamilton (Dundee)
3. Eric Caldow, captain (Rangers)
4. Paddy Crerand (Celtic)
5. Ian Ure (Dundee)
6. Jim Baxter (Rangers)
7. Ralph Brand (Rangers)
8. John White (Tottenham Hotspur)
9. Ian St John (Liverpool)
10. Denis Law (Torino)
11. Hugh Robertson (Dundee)

Wembley via Exeter, or Norwich

WHERE Bonnie Prince Charlie (a promising inside-left, by all accounts) failed in 1745-46 (only getting as far as Derby) Scotland fans perfected the art of invading England in the 1960s and 70s.

Because we'd "never had it so good" (we were assured), the extra spending power made travel to Wembley a realistic and greatly enjoyed railway or bus weekend for tens of thousands of Scots.

It was the ultimate away trip. You'd save two bob a week for two years, then blow the lot on the bus or train fare, liver-numbing supplies of booze and maybe, just maybe, a ticket.

Food didn't matter much. Accommodation wasn't even considered.

Train tickets weren't strictly essential either. You could squeeze on to the cattle truck-standard rolling stock with the Scots horde, secure in the knowledge that no guard would be brave enough to check tickets.

The buses were just as easy to get on free, although there were accompanying health hazards. Unlike the trains they had no toilets, but people did the toilet anyway. Football had a distinct aroma in those days.

The big problem was a ticket for the ground. This was serious. Large numbers of Metropolitan Police, who never had a sense of humour about such things, made illegal entry to Wembley a daunting prospect.

The SFA got some tickets to distribute, but getting one wasn't easy. Many a Scot who went on a dozen Wembley jaunts never saw an official SFA ticket.

There were other avenues. One ruse that hovers somewhere between urban legend and "Aye, God's honest – ah did that" anecdote was the provincial English club route.

The idea was that in the months prior to the Wembley weekend you applied by post to join the official Norwich City FC supporters' club. Or Gillingham, or Swindon, or Exeter. Which club it was didn't matter.

English clubs got tickets dished out to them, which they in turn distributed to their official supporters' clubs.

These "official" England fans were (popular Scottish belief had it) too scared to mingle with the gathering of the clans in London, so only the ever-so-clever Scotland-based fans (newly joined, and having never attended a game at Carrow Road, Priestfield, or the County Ground) took up the offer.

It worked. Some of the time. Maybe.

■ **Right: Wembley Stadium, stuffed with die-hard members of the Exeter City Supporters' Club (Glasgow branch).**

THE natural Scotland-England order was, at last, restored in the 1960s.

Scotland hadn't beat the English at Hampden for a long 25 years – since Hearts' elegant inside-right Tommy Walker got the only goal in the 1938 game (this was the first goal ever to be seen live on UK television).

But 1962 ended the drought.

The 2-0 victory was, if anything, a let-off for those in white shirts.

This photo shows an early Ian St John (No.9) shot in that 1962 game, but it just slipped past England keeper Ron Springett's post.

But it was a signpost for the direction the game would be taking.

■ **Team v England, April 14th, 1962:**
1. **Bill Brown (Tottenham Hotspur)**
2. **Alex Hamilton (Dundee)**
3. **Eric Caldow, captain (Rangers)**
4. **Paddy Crerand (Celtic)**
5. **Billy McNeill (Celtic)**
6. **Jim Baxter (Rangers)**
7. **Alex Scott (Rangers)**
8. **John White (Tottenham Hotspur)**
9. **Ian St John (Liverpool)**
10. **Denis Law (Torino)**
11. **Davie Wilson (Rangers)**

■ Two views of Davie Wilson's opening goal in the 1962 game.

The photo above is an early attempt at a newspaper graphic showing how Wilson's shot arrowed into the net. The pic on the right, taken from behind the goal at the exact same time as the photo above, shows England centre-half Peter Swan's despairing attempt to keep the shot out.

Later in 1962 Swan was to play in the fateful match in which he and two of his Sheffield Wednesday teammates bet on their team to lose a league game to Ipswich – which they did, 2-0. The betting scam was eventually uncovered and Swan served four months in jail and was given a life ban from the game, though he returned to play for Wednesday in 1972.

Alf Ramsay once said that a defender of Swan's quality would have been "first pick" for his 1966 World Cup squad.

■ **Then we got a penalty. These are another two very different views of Eric Caldow's win-clinching and expertly-placed spot-kick, that sparked scenes of wild celebrations around Hampden.**

The pic above is a photo taken on the day, from the main stand at Hampden. Caldow is just out of shot to the left. The photo on the right, taken in 1966, is of Eric in his pub, the Eric Caldow Bar in Hamilton, with a painting of his famous penalty that was done by one of the regulars at the bar and presented to him.

Skipper Eric Caldow makes
certain of Scotland's first victory
in 25 years at Hampden
Park, with a penalty against
England. Score: Scotland 2, England 0.

Lanarkshires Greatest
Sport
MICK MITCHELL
BURNBANK

VACUUM CHIMNEY SWEEP
D. SMITH

MARTALO'S

THE players were called out of the dressing room, by popular demand, to do a lap of honour.

The 1962 game carried more weight than even a normal Scotland-England encounter. This was payback for the previous year's debacle at Wembley (see page 90).

This game restored pride not just to the football team, but to the nation itself.

For a significant proportion of Scottish people, Scotland's national identity is enmeshed with the fortunes of our football team.

The terrible defeat of the previous year had thrown the population into a 12-month depression. We'd fallen out of love with the game a little bit. The national side wasn't discussed as much in pubs and workplaces, or if it was there was a self-deprecating, comedy element to the talk.

But that changed with the Hampden 1962 game. We could again hold our tartan-tammied heads high.

England would soon be off to the World Cup finals in Chile, while we hadn't qualified. But at least we knew they wouldn't win the thing.

■ The crowd at that England game at Hampden in 1962 was 132,431. They played a part in the game. The supporters lucky enough to get a ticket for this (or any) Scotland game have a responsibility. The Hampden Roar is famous throughout world football, but it doesn't just happen. It requires the full strength of the lungs, vocal cords, and most importantly the attitude, of every supporter present. It is a powerful weapon we have in our national football armoury. It is easy to bring out the roar when things on the pitch are going

well, but it also sometimes has to come out when it is most needed. Football fans create atmosphere. The noise they make is fuel for the spirit and confidence of the players. A crowd fervently behind its team can make players run faster, reach high balls, and win tackles they might not otherwise have won. It can also intimidate weaker members of the opposition. The roar is a power that belongs to the fans. When the team needs them, when things aren't going so well, Scotland fans have a duty to use that power.

A SMALL, perhaps almost insignificant, last point on the Scotland v. England game of 1962. But one worth making.

The photo on the right shows a header by Johnny Haynes (he is on ground) that hit the bar. The ball then bounced down on to Scotland keeper Bill Brown's goal line, then up into the air for Billy McNeill to head clear.

The rule is that a goal is scored only when all of the football has crossed all of the line. This has always been the rule. Not bounced on the line, and not just some of the ball crossing the line. All of the ball, all of the line.

This was four years before a Russian linesman altered the rule. On this 1962 occasion, a goal wasn't given.

■ There is something of an optical illusion in this photograph, with the placement of the strong shadows not helping. It looks like the goal-line wavers badly off the straight. It is sometimes difficult to tell exactly what is going on in 60-year-old photos, which adds to their charm.

SCOTLAND'S 1963 win over England at Wembley was a great occasion, though it came at a heavy cost to Eric Caldow.

This was the first international to be played since Wembley had roofs put over the terraces behind the goals. The Scotland fans took full advantage of this new echo chamber, making a hell of a racket!

■ **Left: Scotland centre-half Ian Ure duels with England's Bryan Douglas.**

■ **Right: Ian St John raises his arms in celebration as Jim Baxter (just in sight behind England left-back Gerry Byrne) places a shot round debutant Gordon Banks into the net for Scotland's first goal.**

ENGLAND's Bobby Smith put in such a late challenge on Eric Caldow in the 1963 game that it was almost an off-the-ball incident. It was as clear a sending off as you could ever see.

Caldow, Scotland's captain, had his leg broken in two places and clearly could take no further part in the game. Indeed, he would never play for Scotland again. Smith came back on to the pitch after treatment in the dressing room and limped about being loudly booed by the Scotland fans at every touch.

Scotland played with 10 men for the rest of the game, and were reduced to nine for part of the second half when Ian St John also sustained an injury. Substitutes weren't a part of the game in those days.

It wasn't until 1966 that subs were allowed in Scottish games.

Archie Gemmill was the very first domestic Scottish sub, replacing centre-half Jim Clunie after 23 minutes of St Mirren's League Cup tie against Clyde on August 23, 1966. Subs' names had to be on the team lines, which may seem obvious now but wasn't then. Strictly, only the named man could come on.

However, for that first season, 1966-67, the sub could only be used if they replaced an injured player.

This wasn't an issue in the first game where a sub was seen. It was well documented that Clunie had been struggling to play and he lasted less than a quarter of the game.

However, the "for injuries only" rule was widely abused. Players would go down – it was often claimed – at the command of their managers. It became unworkable, and very unpopular with the supporters. Tactical substitutions were allowed from the beginning of the 1967-68 season.

From 1972-73, two subs were allowed in Scotland, although in England the one-sub-only rule remained in place until, quite surprisingly, the 1987-88 season.

The argument for subs was simple – spectators paid to see a proper game of football, not a one-sided game of 11 v 10 or sometimes 11 v 9.

The argument against substitutes, however, isn't so easy to explain. There was certainly a feeling that "this is the way it is because this is the way it has been for 100 years". The blazers of the SFA were never at the forefront of change in the game.

There was also an "it's a man's game" attitude.

Foreigners (the subs rule was embraced on the Continent first) might roll about at the slightest touch, but we didn't do that in the British game.

We got on with it, playing through very bad injuries at times.

■ **Right: The injury to Eric Caldow causes a good deal of concern as England's Spurs centre-forward Smith (left) is also treated.**

THE 1967 game is a more celebrated occasion (see page 176) for the fact that we became world champions – and Slim Jim's keepie-ups. You can see why that would be.

But 1963 was a more complete footballing performance. Scotland played most of this game with 10 men whereas the '67 match is slightly tainted because England's Jack Charlton, with a broken toe, was a passenger (substitutions were even slower to be adopted in the international game).

In 1963, though, Dave Mackay, John White and, especially, Jim Baxter completely controlled the game. It was a commanding team performance, a football lesson. Quite apart from his two goals, this was probably Baxter's finest game in a Scotland strip.

■ **Left: Willie Henderson and Davie Wilson celebrate the 1963 victory.**

■ **Right: Then they parade the Lion Rampant round the pitch, with Jim Baxter in the background.**

■ **Team v England, April 6th, 1963:**
1. **Bill Brown (Tottenham Hotspur)**
2. **Alex Hamilton (Dundee)**
3. **Eric Caldow, captain (Rangers)**
4. **Dave MacKay (Tottenham Hotspur)**
5. **Ian Ure (Dundee)**
6. **Jim Baxter (Rangers)**
7. **Willie Henderson (Rangers)**
8. **John White (Tottenham Hotspur)**
9. **Ian St John (Liverpool)**
10. **Denis Law (Manchester United)**
11. **Davie Wilson (Rangers)**

■ Denis Law in typically combative action against Maurice Norman while playing for the Rest of the World in a game at Wembley to mark 100 years of the Football Association. England won 2-1, but Denis scored the RotW's goal.

■ Rest of World Team v England, October 23, 1963:
1. Lev Yashin (USSR)
   Sub. Milutin Soskic (Yugoslavia)
2. Djalma Santos (Brazil)
   Sub. Luis Eyzaguirre (Chile)
3. Karl-Heinz Schnellinger (West Germany)
4. Svatopluk Pluskal (Czechoslovakia)
5. Jan Popluhar (Czechoslovakia)
6. Josef Masopust (Czechoslovakia)
   Sub. Jim Baxter (Scotland)
7. Raymond Kopa (France)
8. Denis Law (Scotland)
9. Alfredo di Stefano, captain (Argentina)
   Sub. Uwe Seeler (West Germany)
10. Eusebio (Portugal)
    Sub. Ferenc Puskas (Spain)
11. Francisco Gento (Spain)

■ England Team:
1. Gordon Banks (Leicester City)
2. Jimmy Armfield, captain (Blackpool)
3. Ray Wilson (Huddersfield Town)
4. Gordon Milne (Liverpool)
5. Maurice Norman (Tottenham Hotspur)
6. Bobby Moore (West Ham United)
7. Terry Paine (Southampton)
8. Jimmy Greaves (Tottenham Hotspur)
9. Bobby Smith (Tottenham Hotspur)
10. George Eastham (Arsenal)
11. Bobby Charlton (Manchester United)
Subs (unused):
Tony Waiters (Blackpool)
Ken Shellito (Chelsea)
Ron Flowers (Wolverhampton Wanderers)
Tony Kay (Everton)
Joe Baker (Arsenal)

■ **Left: Davie Wilson gets in a cross during a magnificent 6-2 thrashing of Spain in a World Cup qualifier in the Bernabeu stadium in Madrid – just a year before the Spanish won the European Championship.**

■ **Team v Spain, June 13th, 1963:**
1. Adam Blacklaw (Burnley)
2. Billy McNeill (Celtic)
3. Davie Holt (Hearts)
4. Frank McLintock (Leicester City)
5. Ian Ure (Dundee)
6. Jim Baxter (Rangers)
7. Willie Henderson (Rangers)
8. Dave Gibson (Leicester City)
9. Ian St John (Liverpool)
10. Denis Law, captain (Manchester United)
11. Davie Wilson (Rangers)

■ **Right: Denis Law is up highest in the 1964 Home International against Wales in Cardiff.**

■ **Team v Wales, October 3rd, 1964:**
1. Campbell Forsyth (Kilmarnock)
2. Alex Hamilton (Dundee)
3. Jim Kennedy (Celtic)
4. John Greig (Rangers)
5. Ron Yeats (Liverpool)
6. Jim Baxter (Rangers)
7. Jimmy Johnstone (Celtic)
8. Dave Gibson (Leicester City)
9. Steve Chalmers (Celtic)
10. Denis Law, captain (Manchester United)
11. Jimmy Robertson (Tottenham Hotspur)

136

IN 1964, Scotland were aiming for their third successive victory over England for the first time since 1884.

As was customary at the time, the team was announced a couple of days before the game, and posed for photos at St Mirren's Love Street Park, where they had been training.

They were happy, relaxed, and up for a laugh with the assembled reporters and photographers.

There was even time for a bit of banter with boss (part-time, and paid just £1,000 a year.) Ian McColl, the former Rangers half-back.

It all looked good.

■ Back, from left: Hamilton, Kennedy, Greig,
Forsyth, Yeats (reserve), McNeill.
Front: Henderson, White,
Gilzean, Law, Wilson,
Baxter.

138

■ And it turned out very good! Alan Gilzean gets up to powerfully head home a Davie Wilson corner for the only goal of the game.

140

■ John White carved the defence apart but hit the outside of the post on this occasion.

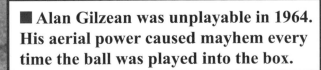

■ Alan Gilzean was unplayable in 1964.
His aerial power caused mayhem every
time the ball was played into the box.

AN SFA spokesman said the 1964 demand was greater than for any other international since the war. He claimed they could have sold 500,000 tickets.

There was a postal ballot that stipulated only applications on postcards (not letters) would be considered.

Anyone asking for more than two tickets would be instantly disqualified.

Applications had to be in the SFA's hands by November 18th the previous year, fully five months before the match.

■ **Left: Andy Stewart leads the pre-match singing.**

■ **Right: Hampden was crammed with an all-ticket 133,245 crowd (134,000 had been sold but it was a very wet day).**

■ There was no segregation, but very little violence. Lots of England supporters attended and could hold up the cross of St George, or a young lady could display a hand-made sign proclaiming her admiration for Gordon Banks, without fear.

■ **Willie Henderson was man of the match, giving Ray Wilson, the Huddersfield Town left-back who was about**

to be sold to Everton – and who, two years later, would be a World Cup-winner – the worst 90 minutes of his career.

■ A photo that almost puts the viewer into the arena with Denis Law.

He has been flagged offside, but Denis, in typical fashion, doesn't give up. He plays to the whistle, and just a little bit beyond – just in case.

He is ready to pounce on any mistake, or perhaps force a mistake, from Gordon Banks.

■ Just as had happened two years previously, the crowd refused to leave the Hampden slopes until Billy McNeill brought the team back out to do a lap of honour. It was a cold, windy, rainy – and glorious day!

■ Right: This was fully quarter of an hour after the final whistle, but barely any spectators had left the ground.

■ Team v England, April 11th, 1964:
1. Campbell Forsyth (Kilmarnock)
2. Alex Hamilton (Dundee)
3. Jim Kennedy (Celtic)
4. John Greig (Rangers)
5. Billy McNeill, captain (Celtic)
6. Jim Baxter (Rangers)
7. Willie Henderson (Rangers)
8. John White (Tottenham Hotspur)
9. Alan Gilzean (Dundee)
10. Denis Law (Manchester United)
11. Davie Wilson (Rangers)

THIS was a greatly
celebrated event, with
much rejoicing on the
terraces. But the crowd was
remarkably well behaved
and allowed the players
a full lap of honour with
just a few "break-ins" (as a
supporter invading the pitch
was then known).

There were no fences
on the track-side walls,
and a only a scattering of
policemen compared to the
huge numbers who would
be required for international
matches in later years.
There were more first aid
men than polis.

Perhaps supporters had
more self control in those
days, or were able to handle
their drink better.

Perhaps it was the more
robust policing that did the
trick. The "break-ins" on
the right have been grabbed
by what was then known
as "the scruff of the neck".
Today the term would be:
"police brutality".

SCOTLAND was blessed with two great captains arising almost simultaneously in the 1960s, Billy McNeill at Celtic and John Greig at Rangers.

They locked horns at club level but these two inspirational players shared a friendship off the pitch and always had a great deal of respect for each other.

They combined their leadership qualities, and great footballing skills, effectively for the national team.

■ **Left: Billy captains Scotland against England in 1964.**

■ **Right: John Greig's finest hour in a Scotland shirt – although he was actually wearing an Italy shirt by the time this photo was taken!**

THE World Cup Qualifier against Italy, on November 9th, 1965, was a biggie.

One thing that all Scottish football fans learn, sometimes without even being told, is that players from warm countries don't like it up 'em.

Or, to be more precise, they won't be able to cope with horizontal rain arrowing across a Hampden pitch, whipped on its way by an ice-edged wind that can cut a fancy-dan Latin footballer in half if it hits them at the correct angle.

We allowed the Italians to train at Hampden the night before the game, but arranged for a freezing Glasgow fog to descend upon them. This, we reckoned, would sort them out.

They, in turn, did their part by donning silly bobble hats and looking extremely uncomfortable while doing awkward-looking arm-waving exercises.

We knew then that we could beat this lot. We were reassured in this opinion when the Italians ran out wearing tracksuit bottoms before the actual game.

WE needed a hero for that Italy game, and John Greig stepped forward.

It was a famous victory that made Scotland's task to get to the World Cup of 1966 clear. Having lost surprisingly (and very disappointingly) 2-1 to Poland at Hampden, we had to beat Italy twice. This 1-0 win was the first hurdle.

The scene was set for one of Scotland's great "obsession games".

■ **Left: We knew all about Greig's determination and strength, it is evident as he and keeper Bill Brown joust with England centre-forward Barry Bridges during the 2-2 draw at Wembley in 1965.**

■ **Right: The Italy game. John Greig, on the ground wearing No.2, is mobbed by team-mates after his late goal (an 88th-minute one-two with Jim Baxter then a left-foot finish) that sparked wild scenes of celebration.**

■ **Team v England, April 10th, 1965:**
1. Bill Brown (Tottenham Hotspur)
2. Alex Hamilton (Dundee)
3. Eddie McCreadie (Chelsea)
4. Pat Crerand (Manchester United)
5. Billy McNeill, captain (Celtic)
6. John Greig (Rangers)
7. Willie Henderson (Rangers)
8. Bobby Collins (Leeds United)
9. Ian St John (Liverpool)
10. Denis Law (Manchester United)
11. Davie Wilson (Rangers)

■ **Team v Italy, November 9th, 1965:**
1. Bill Brown (Tottenham Hotspur)
2. John Greig (Rangers)
3. David Provan (Rangers)
4. Bobby Murdoch (Celtic)
5. Ron McKinnon (Rangers)
6. Jim Baxter, captain (Sunderland)
7. Willie Henderson (Rangers)
8. Billy Bremner (Leeds United)
9. Alan Gilzean (Tottenham Hotspur)
10. Neil Martin (Sunderland)
11. John Hughes (Celtic)

Obsession games

FROM time to time a game of football comes along that entirely grips Scotland's imagination. We become obsessed. Newspapers, radio and TV talk of little else. Line-ups and tactics become the only topics of conversation across kitchen tables and in pubs.

Indeed, Scotland is a world leader in the art of big game obsession. We could give other nations lessons in how to do it properly.

So it was with that away game against Italy. We were mesmerised.

Photographers were despatched to record every step the players took in the lead-up to the game, which was set for December 7th.

■ **Left: December 2nd – the team play head tennis at the Inverclyde training facility at Largs.**

■ **Right – December 5th – the team fly out from Prestwick, and Willie Henderson's jaw drops in shock and dismay as he learns Denis Law is O-U-T out!**

See Naples and die

NO ONE with any sense expected Scotland to go to Italy's traditional southern fortress, the Stadio San Paolo in Naples, where the Azzurri crowd is the most partisan, and actually win.

Unsurprisingly, we all did expect a win.

We reckoned that despite being very much second favourites to an Italian side filled with superstars we could qualify for England 1966 by beating them, just as we'd beaten them at Hampden.

We didn't, of course, we lost 3-0.

A headline was pasted over the game that would stay with Scotland games for ever more: "Brave Scots Go Down Fighting".

The interest in this "obsession game" was incredible. The SFA approached the Scottish League with a request to cancel all First Division matches on the Saturday before the game. And, surprisingly, the League agreed – although as it turned out a big freeze put almost every match in Scotland off anyway.

Both BBC and ITV screened the game live, a new thing for Scotland fans. But the Tuesday afternoon kick-off caused a problem for employers. Some workplaces suffered up to 20% absenteeism.

TV-hire shops had crowds five and six deep outside their city centre shops.

Pubs scrambled to get a TV set up (a pub with a TV was a rarity in 1965) but those that managed it reported double or triple takings.

Thousands of schoolboys feigned upset stomachs, tickly coughs, and headaches – and a good many just missed afternoon classes without explanation, resigning themselves to being belted the next day.

All of Scotland was at fever pitch. These were heady times to be a Scotland fan and set the pattern for what would follow 13 years later in the run-up to Argentina 1978.

Law, Baxter, and Henderson were injured for the game in Naples, and Liverpool's towering Ron Yeats wore the No.9 shirt but played at his usual centre-half.

The game started well. In an unfamiliar all-white strip, Scotland held the much-vaunted Italians to 0-0 until almost half-time, although we were pinned back in our own goal area for much of it. But then a cross eluded Eddie McCreadie and Bologna winger Ezio Pascutti tucked it away.

The lads tried hard, and had a few long-range efforts that went close, but further goals from Facchetti and Mora sealed the deal.

It was the result most of the rest of Europe had expected, but bookies in Scotland reported record takings from lost 3 to 1-odds bets that confident Scotsmen had placed on their side to win.

■ A cross from far out on the right comes in from Inter Milan all-time-great Giacinto Facchetti. His club team-mate, Alessandro Mazzola (making a leap in this photo), didn't get a touch on it – neither did Blacklaw, McKinnon, or Bremner – and it ended up in the net to make the score 2-0 and effectively kill the game.

The dream of winning the World Cup on English soil was over.

■ Team v Italy, December 7th, 1965:
1. Adam Blacklaw (Burnley)
2. David Provan (Rangers)
3. Eddie McCreadie (Chelsea)
4. Bobby Murdoch (Celtic)
5. Ron McKinnon (Rangers)
6. John Greig, captain (Rangers)
7. Jim Forrest (Rangers)
8. Billy Bremner (Leeds United)
9. Ron Yeats (Liverpool)
10. Charlie Cooke (Dundee)
11. John Hughes (Celtic)

Oor Denis

A SCOTS crowd will thrill to see a tanner-ba' winger, a man with skill and pace who can shimmy round a full-back to fire in a dangerous cross. They also love a half-back who can find a defence-splitting pass. They admire an inside-forward who can instantly pull down and control a high ball.

Scottish fans are steeped in football. Most were raised with a ball at their feet so know exactly what the game is all about.

What they demand above all else is passion, a pride in the shirt, a wholehearted, full-blooded, never-say-die effort from their players.

That's why Denis Law is revered.

He is Scotland's (shared) all-time top goal-scorer, which helps in the hero stakes. And he always made himself available for the national side where others had been known to pull out of a midweek pool yet play for their club side on the Saturday.

But what really sets Denis aside is that he played every Scotland game as if it was his last, and his life was staked on the result. If there was a sniff of a ball to be won, Denis went for it – brave as the lion on his shirt, boots flying, elbows out. He didn't hold back, didn't ask for mercy, and gave none in return.

Denis wanted to, needed to, demanded to win games of football.

■ You'll have had to turn your book on its side for this photo. Denis jousts with Wales' man mountain John Charles at Ninian Park in 1962.

DENIS is Scotland's joint top scorer, with 30. He overtook Hughie Gallacher with his 24th goal in 1966, and Denis's tally was equalled by Kenny Dalglish in 1984.

The Lawman's stats include two goals in a game that didn't finish.

Scotland were playing a "friendly" at Hampden against Austria on May 8th, 1963. English ref James Finney sent Horst Nemec off on 26 minutes for spitting at him while claiming Davie Wilson's second goal was offside.

Denis added another two and Austria had pulled a goal back, but then Erich Hof launched a high challenge at Willie Henderson.

Finney sent him off too but he refused to go, with the Austrian backroom team on the sideline pushing their player back on to the field.

It was the Wild West after that, with the Austrians hurtling into leg-breaker challenges. Denis flattened Anton Linhart after being kicked and the ref sent the Scot off with 11 minutes left.

It descended into chaos and referee Finney abandoned the whole thing.

The goals count on Denis's Scotland tally, but when he scored six for Manchester City against Luton Town in a game that was abandoned due to a downpour, the goals were removed from his record.

City were winning 6–2, but lost the replay 3–1 – although Denis scored the one. It's not every week a player scores seven in a cup-tie and ends up on the losing side.

■ Perhaps the most Denis Law-like goal Denis ever scored in a Scotland shirt. It was the Auld Enemy game of 1966 at Hampden. Denis made a prodigious leap to meet a Willie Johnston corner, contorting his body like a steel spring to force maximum power into the header. Banks barely saw it go in.

THE Auld Enemy game of 1966 is the perfect illustration of the frustrations of the 1960s Scotland team.

The line-ups are below. England won 4-3, but man for man, the southerners don't look much better than us. They have good players, of course. Even the most biased Scot would admit Bobby Charlton and Bobby Moore were decent.

But do you prefer Billy Bremner in midfield, or Nobby Stiles? Would you select Denis Law as striker, or Roger Hunt? Any team at that time would have to consider Jimmy Johnstone and Jim Baxter, they were world-class players.

Yet England lifted the World Cup a few months later, while Scotland could only look on. Football is, indeed, a game of narrow margins.

■ **Team v England, April 2nd, 1966:**
1. Bobby Ferguson (Kilmarnock)
2. John Greig, captain (Rangers)
3. Tommy Gemmell (Celtic)
4. Bobby Murdoch (Celtic)
5. Ronnie McKinnon (Rangers)
6. Jim Baxter (Sunderland)
7. Jimmy Johnstone (Celtic)
8. Denis Law (Manchester United)
9. Willie Wallace (Hearts)
10. Billy Bremner (Leeds United)
11. Willie Johnston (Rangers)

■ **England:**
1. Gordon Banks (Leicester City)
2. George Cohen (Fulham)
3. Keith Newton (Blackburn Rovers)
4. Nobby Stiles (Manchester United)
5. Jack Charlton (Leeds United)
6. Bobby Moore (West Ham United)
7. Alan Ball (Blackpool)
8. Roger Hunt (Liverpool)
9. Bobby Charlton (Manchester United)
10. Geoff Hurst (West Ham United)
11. John Connelly (Manchester United)

THOUGH sadly not taking part in World Cup 1966, Scotland were in high demand as pre-tournament opponents.

The Portuguese, led by the much-admired Eusebio, came to visit in June.

The Scots, with eight Anglos in the starting line-up, gave a fairly good account of themselves at a sunny Hampden before going down to a late header from giant centre-forward Jose Torres.

■ **Team v Portugal, June 18th, 1966:**
1. Bobby Ferguson (Kilmarnock)
2. Willie Bell (Leeds United)
3. Eddie McCreadie (Chelsea)
4. John Greig, captain (Rangers)
5. Jackie McGrory (Kilmarnock)
6. Billy Bremner (Leeds United)
7. Alex Scott (Everton)
8. Charlie Cooke (Chelsea)
9. Alex Young (Everton)
   Sub 46 min, Stevie Chalmers (Celtic)
10. Jim Baxter (Sunderland)
11. Jackie Sinclair (Leicester City)

Slightly Brazilian

EVERYONE in Scotland is slightly Brazilian. The South Americans play the game the way we'd like to play it, with style, skill, and panache. They call it the "jogo bonito", which, translated into Scots is "bonny gemme". I don't know what the Portuguese word for "gallus" is but there probably is one, and it will be used to describe players who have a bit of Scottishness about them.

The Brazilians came to Hampden in the summer of 1966 for their first ever meeting with Scotland, another team needing a World Cup warm-up. This was just a fortnight before Brazil were to kick off the England '66 tournament as cup holders for the past eight years.

Stevie Chalmers scored for the Brazilians in dark blue after just 45 seconds, though the Brazilians in yellow equalised on 16 minutes.

All in all, a draw with the favourites for the World Cup about to begin wasn't a bad result, but we should have beaten them on the balance of play.

Slim Jim Baxter was clearly the man of the match – no mean feat in a game that had Pele, Zito, Jairzinho, and Gerson also playing.

■ Team v Brazil, June 25th, 1966:
1. Bobby Ferguson (Kilmarnock)
2. John Greig, captain (Rangers)
3. Willie Bell (Leeds United)
4. Billy Bremner (Leeds United)
5. Ron McKinnon (Rangers)
6. John Clark (Celtic)
7. Alex Scott (Everton)
8. Charlie Cooke (Chelsea)
9. Stevie Chalmers (Celtic)
10. Jim Baxter (Sunderland)
11. Peter Cormack (Hibernian)

■ **Right: Stevie Chalmers bursts on to a Baxter pass and lashes the ball into the roof of the net for the game's opening goal.**

THE first full international of 1967 was the Auld Enemy clash at Wembley. The Scotland players gathered at the North British Hotel in Glasgow on Thursday, April 13th, ready to travel south for the game two days later.

Some were already seasoned internationals. Others, like Ronnie Simpson, pictured left being welcomed by new team boss Bobby Brown (see page 346) and, right, by John Greig (watch where you're putting your feet, lads) had never played in a full Scotland match.

Immortality beckoned.

Wembley 1967

THE win of 1963 was more comprehensive, the Hampden victory of '64 was a better performance. But 1967 stands out as the most Scottish way to have beaten the English.

Crucially, Scotland were very much the underdogs, having been completely written off by the English press. If anyone was to halt the 19-game unbeaten run of the world champions, they reckoned, it wouldn't be a team in dark blue shirts.

And Scotland weren't able to field the team that new-in-the-job manager Bobby Brown had wanted. It was to have been centred upon the talents of Celtic's Jimmy Johnstone, who was in superb form that season. The plan was to have him run at English full-backs, Wilson and Cohen, who Brown thought were vulnerable to the talents of a winger of Johnstone's type. But Jinky was injured in Celtic's European Cup Semi-Final against Dukla Prague.

Whatever the plan, the 1967 result was – as all Scots know – a 3-2 win that could have, and probably should have, been by a much wider margin.

Jack Charlton limped about on the wing for most of the match, having broken his toe in a challenge with Bobby Lennox. But he still managed to score a goal. Banks pulled off a miraculous backward-diving save to get to a Law chip. And Scotland deliberately kept the ball, preferring to stroke it around in midfield rather than score more.

But it was, all in all, a good victory.

■ **Denis Law's goal.**

The pain of thinking 'What if?'

AS often happens with big games, myths sprung up around Wembley 1967. It wasn't until 2001 that the full footage was made public. It wasn't on TV on the day (the only Scotland-England game of the 1960s not shown live on the BBC or ITV).

Jim Baxter did play keepie-up, briefly. But he didn't sit on the ball, as had often been claimed. Baxter and Bremner threw "Jimmy Clitheroe" jibes at Alan Ball, which is funny but didn't affect the way Ball played – he would be used to intimidatory tactics as a mouthy, overly-confident young player in the tough environment of the English First Division.

There wasn't an immediate pitch invasion, either. The players of both sides lined up for the National Anthem (as was customary at the time) before walking off down the tunnel. It was only then that the real pitch invasion (and turf collections) began.

The myths aren't the important thing. In the years since, any talk of Wembley 1967 has centred around those "taking the mickey" legends. We should stop talking about it like this. It's the wrong way to look at it. Taking the mickey isn't what wins silverware.

It wasn't a massacre, but it wasn't a fluke. It was a close game. The important thing is that we were good enough to play a tough, high-pressure 90 minutes and beat the World Cup holders on their own pitch.

That 1967 performance throws up tantalising questions about what might have happened if we'd gone to the previous summer's World Cup Finals with Law, Baxter, Bremner, and Johnstone on top form?

What if Scotland had qualified in place of Italy, who had edged us out? They were in Group 4, with the USSR, Chile, and North Korea.

Chile weren't the force they'd been at their own 1962 tournament. The Soviets were a good team and qualified with three wins. But the North Koreans got through to the knock-out stages with just three points, thanks mainly to a 1-0 surprise win over the Italians.

Could we have qualified from that group?

North Korea played Portugal in the first knockout round, which was a quarter-final as World Cups didn't have so many rounds in those days.

If Scotland had been in that game, at a Goodison Park packed full of fervent Scotsmen, could we have beaten Eusebio's team? The Koreans were, after all, 3-0 up at one point before losing 5-3.

Portugal's next game was England in the semis. We had just proved we could beat England.

And the final against West Germany? We played them at Hampden in May 1964 and drew 2-2. The same score England held the Germans to over 90 minutes before winning in extra time, aided by a very questionable decision from a Russian linesman.

It isn't too much a stretch to see us winning it.

■ **Team v England, April 15th, 1967:**
1. Ronnie Simpson (Celtic)
2. Tommy Gemmell (Celtic)
3. Eddie McCreadie (Chelsea)
4. John Greig, captain (Rangers)
5. Ronnie McKinnon (Rangers)
6. Jim Baxter (Sunderland)
7. Willie Wallace (Celtic)
8. Billy Bremner (Leeds United)
9. Jim McCalliog (Sheffield Wednesday)
10. Denis Law (Manchester United)
11. Bobby Lennox (Celtic)

■ **Willie Wallace turns the ball around England's Martin Peters in the unofficial 1967 World Championship game.**

The XI who played this game never took to the field for Scotland again, just as the XI that became known as the Wembley Wizards in 1928 never played for Scotland again.

Perhaps we should be more consistent when we find a winning blend?

■ **Ian Ure and Ronnie McKinnon challenge Northern Ireland's Derek Dougan at Windsor Park, 1967.**

SCOTLAND'S next competitive game, which was Windsor Park, Belfast, was one of our intermittent (and inexplicable) bad days.

This was a Northern Ireland side inspired by George Best, and served very well by the formidable aerial prowess of Derek Dougan up front, and a young Pat Jennings in goal. Bobby Brown slated his players' performances in the post-match interviews, although was too polite to name names.

Coventry City's Dave Clements scored (above) after Best had torn the entire right side of the Scots team to shreds. The Irish could have won by more – Scotland had Ronnie Simpson to thank for a miracle save to keep out a well-struck penalty from Middlesbrough's Johnny Crossan.

It would be a very costly loss.

■ Team v N. Ireland, October 21st, 1967:
1. Ronnie Simpson (Celtic)
2. Tommy Gemmell (Celtic)
3. Eddie McCreadie (Chelsea)
4. John Greig, captain (Rangers)
5. Ron McKinnon (Rangers)
6. Ian Ure (Arsenal)
7. Willie Wallace (Celtic)
8. Bobby Murdoch (Celtic)
9. Jim McCalliog (Sheffield Wednesday)
10. Denis Law (Manchester United)
11. Willie Morgan (Burnley)

Glorious failure. Again

THE 1967 and '68 Home Internationals doubled as qualifiers for the 1968 European Championships. Scotland, England, Wales and Northern Ireland playing each other home and away, with the winners of this two-year table going into a play-off with another of the eight group winners across the continent to decide which four nations would eventually make it to the finals in Italy.

The win at Wembley in 1967 was Scotland's away fixture, so the Hampden 1968 Scotland-England game was the return leg and would be the deciding match of the series. Scotland had drawn their first game, away back in October 1966, with Wales, but had (in true Scotland fashion) been leading the group until that 1-0 loss to Northern Ireland (previous page).

So it came down to a Hampden decider. Another obsession game.

Scotland (seven points) had to win while England (eight points, having won all their other games except the 3-2 Wembley loss to Scotland) needed only to draw.

An unprecedented 30,000 travelling support arrived from England to see a game that had captured all of Europe's attention.

The game was set for a frosty February Saturday (winters were colder in those days). The SFA had covered Hampden with 30 tons of straw in the days before the match, so a 125-strong volunteer-force was required to clear the pitch. But a surprise thaw left the ground boggy when the 134,000 sell-out crowd gathered for the game.

It was a win-or-bust situation.

The home side had most of the early play, but England scored first, a rasping Martin Peters shot after 20 minutes. Yogi Hughes equalised before half-time, but huge controversy surrounded a Bobby Lennox "goal" chalked off for a Willie Johnston infringement on Gordon Banks that only the Dutch referee saw.

Scotland performed well and missed several good chances. But England had a lot of pressure too, hitting the woodwork twice. A draw was fair.

But once again, we'd failed to qualify for a major tournament.

If only we'd beaten the Irish we wouldn't have again needed the headline . . . Brave Scots Go Down Fighting.

THE press reaction to the Euro 68 failure was, predictably, savage. Much of it centred round the decision to play Charlie Cooke instead of Jimmy Johnstone against England.

Jinky, the journalists insisted, would have had a field day with his preternatural balance and ability to swiftly change direction on a slippy pitch – though Cooke had been man of the match.

The press – and the crowd – in the 1960s was always quick to criticise players who played for English clubs which greatly annoyed, and saddened, England-based players.

There were many tales of Anglo-Scots saying they felt alienated when they played for their national side, especially if they'd been vying for a place in the team with an alternative who was a Celtic or Rangers star.

Even big names and outstanding players, such as Denis Law, Pat Crerand, and Frank McLintock, have mentioned this over the years. It was even worse if the Anglo had never played for a Scottish team and was something of an unknown to home fans

■ **Ronnie Simpson beat out this Martin Peters effort, but the shot the Englishman scored with was unstoppable.**

■ **Team v England, February 24th, 1968:**
1. **Ronnie Simpson (Celtic)**
2. **Tommy Gemmell (Celtic)**
3. **Eddie McCreadie (Chelsea)**
4. **Billy McNeill (Celtic)**
5. **Ron McKinnon (Rangers)**
6. **John Greig, captain (Rangers)**
7. **Charlie Cooke (Chelsea)**
8. **Billy Bremner (Leeds United)**
9. **John Hughes (Celtic)**
10. **Willie Johnston (Rangers)**
11. **Bobby Lennox (Celtic)**

186

SCOTLAND were drawn in a tough qualifying group for World Cup 1970, with West Germany, Austria, and Cyprus.

It started well. We beat the Austrians 2-1 at Hampden, then trounced Cyprus 5-0 in Nicosia.

The home game against the Germans was a fantastic Scotland performance. A late Bobby Murdoch equaliser thrilled the Hampden faithful after Gerd Muller had given his team a first-half lead against the run of play. West Germany were lucky to get the draw.

■ Left: Alan Gilzean gets between Franz Beckenbauer and Karl-Heinz Schnellinger to challenge West German keeper Horst Walter. Strangely, the ball looks the wrong shape!

■ Right: Jimmy Johnstone beats Bertie Vogts to get in a diving header.

■ Team v West Germany, April 16th, 1969:
1. **Tommy Lawrence (Liverpool)**
2. **Tommy Gemmell (Celtic)**
3. **Eddie McCreadie (Chelsea)**
4. **Bobby Murdoch (Celtic)**
5. **Ron McKinnon (Rangers)**
6. **John Greig (Rangers)**
7. **Jimmy Johnstone (Celtic)**
8. **Billy Bremner, captain (Leeds United)**
9. **Denis Law (Manchester United)**
10. **Alan Gilzean (Tottenham Hotspur)**
11. **Bobby Lennox (Celtic)**
    Sub, 63 min. Charlie Cooke (Chelsea)

■ Scotland v. Northern Ireland, May 1969.

Scotland's worst crowd

SCOTLAND'S worst ever home crowd came amid a run of good results. The attendance at the Home International against Northern Ireland on Tuesday, May 6th, 1969, was 7,483. But on April 16th, 95,951 had thrilled to the West Germany game (previous page).

There was a bus strike in Glasgow on the day of the Norn Iron game, and it had rained heavily all day – one of the west of Scotland's affy drookit nights.

English League clubs were no longer prepared to release players for Saturday internationals in October and November. So the Home International Championship was staged over eight days, after the domestic season, with all matches televised live.

■ **Team v Northern Ireland, May 6th, 1969:**
1. Jim Herriot (Birmingham City)
2. Tommy Gemmell (Celtic)
3. Eddie McCreadie (Chelsea)
4. Billy Bremner, captain (Leeds United)
5. John Greig (Rangers)
6. Pat Stanton (Hibernian)
7. Willie Henderson (Rangers)
8. Bobby Murdoch (Celtic)
9. Colin Stein (Rangers)
10. Denis Law (Manchester United)
11. Charlie Cooke (Chelsea)
    Sub, 75 min. Willie Johnston (Rangers)

Fans clearly decided that watching at home, nice and dry, was better than being at the match and soaked to the skin.

The viewing figures for this 1-1 draw were upwards of 19 million, a record for a Scotland game at the time.

By 1969, most families had a black-and-white TV in the corner of their living room, many of them hired from firms like Radio Rentals. Some posh folk even had a colour set.

Football had been increasingly, though sporadically, shown live throughout the preceding 20 years, but it was only at the end of the '60s that TV chiefs seemed to notice that there was a regular and eager audience for this football thing. They've never let go of the idea since.

The joke around that 1969 Northern Ireland game was that there were more lassies at Hampden's front entrance trying to catch a glimpse of Georgie Best than there were spectators inside the ground.

But not everyone was laughing. The SFA blazers would spend the next 30 years agonising over gate receipts versus TV live coverage fees.

Consistently inconsistent

THE 1960s ended with a bang, a whimper and another "Brave Scots Go Down Fighting" episode.

The whimper was the ending of our nine-game unbeaten run with a 4-1 loss to England at Wembley. The demands of live TV meant the game was a 7.30pm kick off on a Saturday night (Ireland v. Wales, with a 3pm kick-off, was also live that day).

Scotland had a few flurries, especially after Colin Stein scored just before half-time, but were well beaten by an England side said to be eager for revenge after what they saw as "over celebration" after the last clash at Wembley two years before.

The "bang" and the "Brave Scots" games were yet to come. See next pages.

■ **Right: Scotland on the attack at Wembley 1969.**

■ **Team v England, May 10th, 1969:**
1. Jim Herriot (Birmingham City)
2. Tommy Gemmell (Celtic)
3. Eddie McCreadie (Chelsea)
4. Bobby Murdoch (Celtic)
5. Billy McNeill (Celtic)
6. John Greig (Rangers)
7. Willie Henderson (Rangers)
8. Billy Bremner, captain (Leeds United)
9. Colin Stein (Rangers)
10. Alan Gilzean (Tottenham Hotspur)
    Sub, 57 min. Willie Wallace (Celtic)
11. Eddie Gray (Leeds United)

THE "bang" to finish the 1960s was an 8-0 home victory over Cyprus at a sun-kissed, but sparsely-populated, Hampden a week after the England game.

Rangers star Colin Stein, in fine form that season and scoring in his fourth successive international, got four goals.

However, the Cypriots would lose 12-0 to Germany in Essen five days later, which meant the Germans' goal-difference was two better than Scotland's tally.

■ **Left: Bremner leads out the teams for the Cyprus game.**

■ **Right: Cyprus keeper Michalakis Alkiviadis fails, by quite a distance, to get his hands on another shot.**

■ **Team v Cyprus, May 17th, 1969:**
1. **Jim Herriot (Birmingham City)**
2. **Tommy Gemmell (Celtic)**
3. **Eddie McCreadie (Chelsea)**
4. **Billy Bremner, captain (Leeds United)**
5. **Billy McNeill (Celtic)**
6. **John Greig (Rangers)**
7. **Willie Henderson (Rangers)**
8. **Charlie Cooke (Chelsea)**
9. **Colin Stein (Rangers)**
10. **Alan Gilzean (Tottenham Hotspur)**
11. **Eddie Gray (Leeds United)**

QUALIFICATION for the 1970 World Cup came down to playing West Germany in Hamburg. We needed a win, and then at least a point away to Austria. To the team's credit, they gave it their all, doing Scotland proud in difficult surroundings.

This was probably Jimmy Johnstone's best game for his country and he scored after just three minutes.

But Klaus Fichtel equalised before half-time, then Gerd Muller put the Germans ahead on the hour.

Alan Gilzean put us level with a header, but some shady tactics, including a cowardly Muller punch thrown at Billy McNeill in the lead up to the second goal, and Tommy Gemmell being sent off for exchanging kicks with Helmut Haller (though Haller stayed on) did for us. Stan Libuda got a late winner and Mexico 1970 would have to do without Scotland.

The security was a mess, as often happened in those days of looser policing at matches. It looked like half of Germany was on the pitch protesting after the Gemmell-Haller incident, and there was another intimidating pitch invasion at full-time.

■ **Left: Colin Stein is foiled by Sepp Maier.**
■ **Right: Alan Gilzean has just equalised.**

■ **Team v West Germany, October 22nd, 1969:**
1. **Jim Herriot (Birmingham City)**
2. **John Greig (Rangers)**
3. **Tommy Gemmell (Celtic)**
4. **Billy Bremner, captain (Leeds United)**
5. **Ron McKinnon (Rangers)**
6. **Billy McNeill (Celtic)**
7. **Jimmy Johnstone (Celtic)**
8. **Peter Cormack (Hibernian)**
9. **Alan Gilzean (Tottenham Hotspur)**
10. **Colin Stein (Rangers)**
11. **Eddie Gray (Leeds United)**

Every dark blue shirt

SCOTLAND is represented at every level football is played. And when a player – no matter what age or gender, or whether they are paid – pulls on a dark blue shirt they do so in the knowledge that the entire nation is supporting them. Every Scotland player is a hero. Every game for Scotland is an important game.

Under-23 international games were regarded as important by Scotland's national managers once the SFA took responsibility for them following the re-think after the 1958 World Cup Finals. They became the stepping stone to the full international side, and were picked and managed by the national boss.

Under-23s began with a lamentable 6-0 loss to England at Shawfield in 1955 under the auspices of the Scottish Second Eleven Association. The first Under-23 game against a non-UK nation was a 4-1 win over The Netherlands in 1957.

UEFA organised a European Under-23 Championship in 1975 and 1976 with matches the day before European Championship ties for the full teams, which meant a separate Under-23 manager (Andy Roxbirgh) had to be appointed. Under-21s replaced Under-23s from October 1976.

Schoolboy Internationals started in 1911, and Youth Internationals in 1947, confined to home international matches until 1963.

The progression from schools and youth football to the senior game was always a forked path, with many never finding the way. But a lot of young internationals went on to fulfil their potential.

The amateur international series was a firm date on the football calendar for half a century from 1927, and Junior internationals were first played in 1889.

Players stayed amateur because they had well-paid jobs and could afford to play for nothing for Queen's Park, or in the hope they would attract a professional form and a sizeable signing-on fee, something that was not available to transfers between professional clubs.

The SFA did not recognize the women's game until they were persuaded by UEFA in 1972.

■ **Right: Jimmy Bone in the Under-23 game against Wales at Pittodrie in January 1972.**

■ **Under-23 team v Wales, January 25th, 1972:**
1. **Ally Hunter (Kilmarnock)**
2. **John Brownlie (Hibernian)**
3. **Willie Donachie (Manchester City)**
4. **Sandy Jardine, captain (Rangers)**
5. **Willie Young (Aberdeen)**
6. **Martin Buchan (Aberdeen)**
7. **John McGovern (Derby County)**
   Sub, 77 min. Denis McQuade (Partick Thistle)
8. **Lou Macari (Celtic)**
9. **Jimmy Bone (Partick Thistle)**
10. **Kenny Dalglish (Celtic)**
    Sub, 84 min. Ally Brown (Leicester City)
11. **Alex Cropley (Hibernian)**

THE VICTORY SHIELD is the annual tournament for statutory school leaving age pupils, competed for by the home nations. It was raised to Under-15 in 1949 and Under-16 in 2001. Scotland have a proud record, winning it outright 17 times since the war, and sharing it a further 11 times.

Some very famous players got their first taste of international football in these games.

This is Scotland v England at Ibrox in 1966, with a young Kenny Dalglish in the front row, extreme left.

Tommy Craig,had lengthy career in the game, starting with Aberdeen.

Jim Mullen went to West Ham, then had a long career with Partick Thistle, East Stirling, and Dunfermline.

Mike Milligan would play for QoS. Alex Martin played for Motherwell. Freddie Pethard was on Celtic's books, but went on to play several hundred English league games with Cardiff and Torquay.

Goalkeeper Les Donaldson got a Scottish Junior Cup runner-up medal with Linlithgow Rose in 1974 and is still involved with the club. He was for many years manager of the Scottish schools international team, for which he was awarded an MBE in 2002.

■ **Scotland U-15s team v England, May 14th, 1966:**
(Players are identified by their education area)
1. Les Donaldson (Stirlingshire)
2. Mike Milligan (Dumfries)
3. Brian Wilson (Edinburgh)
4. Freddie Pethard (Glasgow)
5. Robert Smith (Fife)
6. Ian Grant (Hamilton)
7. Alex Martin (Midlothian East)
8. Kenny Dalglish (Glasgow)
9. Jim Mullen (Glasgow)
10. Tommy Craig (Glasgow)
11. Richard Menzies (Fife)

AS with the previous page, there is a fascination in tracing the careers of these young internationals. A few become stars, others never appear at all in the senior game.

This is the Scottish Victory Shield team of 1968, before the game with England.

Tom Livingston was on Celtic's books before playing Junior with Ashfield and Pollok.

Brian Laing was with Liverpool, then Hearts and Queen of the South.

Ally Robertson is one of West Brom's great stalwarts, playing well over 500 games as a respected centre-half before moving to Wolves in 1986 and chalking up another 100-plus appearances as captain.

Maitland Pollock played for Walsall, Luton and Portsmouth before finishing his career at home town club QoS.

Alan Robertson made more than 600 League and Cup appearances during a playing and coaching career with Kilmarnock which spanned five decades.

■ **Scotland U-15s team v England, May 12th, 1968:**
1. **Tom Livingston (Glasgow)**
2. **Tom Sinclair (Hamilton)**
3. **Alan Robertson (Kilmarnock)**
4. **Dougie Devlin (Glasgow)**
5. **Ally Robertson (West Lothian)**
6. **Robert Gray (Glasgow)**
7. **Michael Carroll (Aberdeen)**
8. **James McSorley (Hamilton)**
9. **Brian Laing (Midlothian East)**
10. **Maitland Pollock (Dumfries & Galloway)**
11. **Alan Robertson (Motherwell & Wishaw)**

THIS is an age group above the Victory Shield level, the Scotland v England U-18s schoolboys at Ibrox on May 13th, 1967.

Keith MacRae kept goal for Motherwell and Manchester City before moving to play in the USA.

Walter Clarke played for Airdrie.

George Douglas played for Morton, Hamilton Accies and Berwick Rangers.

Jim Fallon played nearly 800 games for Clydebank, before managing the club for three seasons.

Danny McGrain went on to become one of Celtic's all-time greats and win 62 full Scotland caps.

1. Keith MacRae (Lanark)
   Sub John McVean (Buckie)
2. Billy Henderson (Motherwell)
3. Walter Clarke (Airdrie)
4. Danny McGrain (Glasgow)
5. Jim Fallon (Hamilton)
6. James Glover (Airdrie)
7. David Jack (Edinburgh)
8. Brian McAlinden (Glasgow)
9. Alex Findlay (Motherwell)
10. John McAdam (Glasgow)
11. George Douglas (Coatbridge)

■ **Right: England's keeper scrambles a shot round the post in that 1967 game.**

SCOTTISH Schoolboys were identified by their school, again not the club they might be attached to. This 1969 team beat their English counterparts 1-0 at Ibrox.

Ian Letford was a Scottish Junior Cup winner with Cambuslang Rangers before going senior with Dundee United and Stranraer.

Billy Mitchell was with Raith, Celtic, Dunfermline, and Alloa. John Gallacher enjoyed a lengthy career in League football with Queen's Park, Hearts, and Dumbarton.

Iain Phillip had a long career with Crystal Palace, Dundee, Dundee United, Raith Rovers, and Arbroath – winning League Cup-winners' medals with both Dundee clubs.

Tommy Walker, who scored the winning goal that day in 1969, started his career with Arbroath but became an Airdrieonians stalwart, playing more than 300 games during a decade's service.

Ian Donald was a Manchester United player, making four appearances for the Red Devils. He went on to play a handful of games with Partick Thistle and Arbroath. Years later he succeeded his father Dick as chairman of Aberdeen.

■ **Team v England, May 3rd, 1969:**
1. **William Ritchie (Cumnock Academy)**
2. **William Docherty (Greenock High)**
3. **Irwin McIntyre (Johnstone High)**
4. **Tommy Walker (Arboath High)**
5. **John Gallacher (Falkirk High)**
6. **Ian Donald (Robert Gordon's High)**
7. **Doug Devlin (St Augustine's)**
8. **Ian Letford (North Kelvinside)**
9. **William Mitchell (Buckhaven High)**
10. **Iain Phillip (Grove Academy)**
11. **Ian Mason (Cranhill)**

Scotland's women internationals

THE history of the Scottish Women's team is badly under-represented on these pages. I apologise for that. But there aren't any photos of Scottish women's internationals from the black and white era largely because the SFA didn't sanction such things. No member club was allowed to even host a women's club game, never mind an international.

Women's international football in general was in its infancy in the 1970s. Football authorities in most nations had stifled it. The FA in England stipulated a complete ban in 1921 with Scotland following suit.

However in 1971 UEFA recommended that its member associations recognise women's football. The motion was passed by 33 votes to one, Scotland being the one association that voted against.

The Scottish Women's Football Association was formed in 1972 and immediately affiliated to the SFA.

The one international game that I do have good photos of, from 1977, is a very good one.

Scotland had never beaten England, indeed the English had only ever lost two games, both against Sweden. The three previous occasions when Scotland and England had contested the Eric Worthington Challenge Cup had been 3-2, 8-1, and 5-1 losses.

For the 1977 game the English, boasting five members of the all-powerful Southampton side who dominated the Women's FA Cup for the first decade of its existence, were again odds-on favourites.

Scotland's men were to play England at Wembley the following weekend (see page 298) but the women got in first to provide an example of what glorious victory looked like.

Dundee's Downfield Park (home of Junior side Downfield) saw a fantastic 2-1 win.

Scotland started out strongly, forcing a succession of corners, but didn't score until the 35th minute when Liz Creamer got to a Jane Legget ball over the top and beat the keeper with her header.

The English equalised 12 minutes into the second half from a Parker penalty, after Foreman was adjudged to have been fouled in the box.

The winner came late, but was worth waiting for – a deft lob from Scotland's top scorer at club level that season, Marie Blagojevic, on as sub for Creamer.

Ann Squires, a native of Newport-on-Tay who had been tempted south to the great Southampton team of the 1970s, that day became the first Anglo to play for Scotland, taking her place in central defence.

Women's football in Scotland was on the up.

■ **Right: Scotland's Liz Smith punches clear with Marion Barclay (No. 2) standing by if needed.**

■ **Left: England keeper Janet Milner scrambles a cross away with Scotland's Lorraine Spurvey ready to pounce.**

■ Squad for game v England, May 29th, 1977:
Marion Banta (Motherwell)
Sheila Begbie (Edinburgh Dynamos)
Marie Blagojevic (Westhorn United)
Elizabeth Creamer (Dundee Strikers)
Sharon Dobbie (Dundee Strikers)
Helen Leyden (Grangemouth)
Jane Legget (Edinburgh Dynamos)
Margaret McAuley (Westhorn United)
Margaret McGough (Edinburgh Dynamos)
Mary O'Neill (Dundee Strikers)
Agnes Reilly (Westhorn United)
Elizabeth Smith (Motherwell)
Lorraine Spurvey (Dundee Strikers)
Ann Squires (Southampton)
Betty Ure (Westhorn United)
Eleanor Vineski (Motherwell)

■ England squad:
Sue Buckett (Southampton)
Pat Chapman (Southampton)
Linda Coffin (Southampton)
Linda Curle (Lowestoft)
Elizabeth Brigham (St Helens)
Lorraine Dobb (Rangers, Nottingham)
Ellen Foreman (Warminster)
Christine Hutchinson (Wallsend)
Morag Kirkland (Southampton)
Alison Leatherbarrow (Prestatyn)
Jose Lee (Queens Park Rangers)
Sue Lopez (Southampton)
Janet Milner (Darlington)
Carol McClune (Hull)
Sheila Parker (Preston North End)

■ The crowd at that 1977 game was well over 1,000 – many more than had been expected.

SCOTLAND'S amateur internationals used to attract quite a crowd in the 1950s, with the first to be played at Wembley getting 80,000 through the turnstiles. However, the 5,825 at this meeting with England (March 29th, 1958) was so poor that it was the last encounter at England's national stadium.

Scotland won 3-2, with a hat-trick from Queen's Park's Dougie Orr.

Scotland played amateur internationals between 1926 and 1974, and were runners-up to Austria in the 1967 UEFA Amateur Cup.

Famous names such as Donald Ford (11 goals in nine appearances 1965-66) and Peter Lorimer (seven goals in seven games in 1963) played before signing as pros.

Davie Holt (in this line-up) went on to win five full Scottish caps while a Hearts player.

■ **Amateur Team v England, March 29th, 1958:**
John Freebairn (Glasgow University)
Ian Harnett (Queen's Park)
Frank McGregor (Jordanhill Training College)
Bert Cromar (Queen's Park)
Billy Neil (Airdrie)
Davie Holt (Queen's Park)
Dougie Orr (Queen's Park)
Ken McDonald (Hounslow Town)
Andy McEwan (Queen's Park)
Jimmy Robb (Queen's Park)
Ted Perry (Queen's Park)

■ **Left: Scotland keeper John Freebairn clutching a cross.**
   ■ **Right: England goalie Mike Pinner (Pegasus AFC) in a race with Scotland's Andy McEwan and England centre-half Stan Prince (Walthamstow Avenue).**

The League Internationals

IN his autobiography George Young, the Rangers colossus, proudly states that he played 75 games for his country. And he did, 53 internationals and a further 22 for the Scottish League XI.

The Scottish League internationals will be a mystery to anyone under the age of 50. They were games for which only players actually playing in the Scottish Leagues would play XIs from other leagues. This meant players born elsewhere would play for the nation of the club they were signed to. The first English League XI in 1892 contained three Scots playing against their country.

Celtic legend Patsy Gallacher, although born in Donegal and an Ireland international, played two games for Scotland's League XI. Motherwell's gifted winger Bob Ferrier couldn't play for Scotland because he was born in Sheffield. But he played seven games for the Scottish League XI, scoring five goals.

Celtic's Bobby Evans holds the record for Scottish League XI appearances, with 25. Hearts legend Barney Battles Jr got 13 goals in five games between 1928 and 1930.

The League XI matches declined in popularity once the European club competitions arose, but were once very well attended. A crowd of 90,000 saw the Scotland v England League XI clash of 1949.

Annual matches were played against the English and Irish Leagues, and the English Southern League (prior to the First World War). In 1948 the League of Ireland joined the annual fixtures and there were one-off matches against Wales and Denmark and two against Italy.

Denis Law played for the Serie A XI against Scotland in 1961, along with Welshman John Charles, before 67,000 at Hampden and drew 1-1.

Prior to 1926, the Irish match was occasionally staged in Edinburgh, Dundee and Paisley, but thereafter all Inter-League games were at the major Glasgow grounds.

The games declined in popularity from the 1960s, with clubs often pulling players out if they had a big game looming. The death knells were an embarrassing 5-0 defeat by the English at Maine Road in 1974, then a poorly-attended return fixture, the last ever Scotland v England League XI, at Hampden in 1976.

In 1978 and 1980 there were two matches against the Irish League and single games against the League of Ireland and Italy's Serie B.

The idea was briefly resurrected in 1990, when a Scottish League XI played the Scotland international team at Hampden to mark the centenary of the SFL. The League XI won 1-0 with a penalty from Aberdeen's Dutch maestro Hans Gilhaus.

In total, the Scottish League XI played 169 games, 75 of them against the English League.

■ **What's this? Denis Law in an England shirt? The Lawman was playing for the English League against the Italian League in 1960. His side lost 4-2.**

216

■ Aberdeen's Joe Harper scores one of his two goals for the Scottish League against the Irish League at Ibrox in November 1969. Scotland won 5-2, with further goals from Davie Robb, Peter Cormack, and sub Willie Johnston.

The crowd at Ibrox was just 4,400.

■ Team v Irish League, November 19th, 1969:
1. Ally Donaldson (Dundee)
2. Dave Clunie (Hearts)
3. John Greig, captain (Rangers)
4. Eddie Thomson (Hearts)
5. Gerry Sweeney (Morton)
6. Pat Stanton (Hibernian)
7. Peter Cormack (Hibernian)
8. Joe Harper (Aberdeen)
9. Alex Ingram (Ayr United)
    Sub, Willie Johnston (Rangers)
10. Davie Robb (Aberdeen)
11. Eric Stevenson (Hibernian)

■ Crowds were better for League internationals against the English League, but by this point (1969) interest in League Representative games was beginning to wane. The attendance at this match at Hampden, a deserved 3-1 loss to an English side inspired by its captain Alan Ball, was 23,582. Scotland did, however, miss two penalties (Murdoch and Greig) in this game. The photo shows Peter Cormack hitting the post.

■ Team v English League, March 26th, 1969:
1. Jim Cruickshank (Hearts)
2. Willie Callaghan (Dunfermline Athletic)
3. Willie Mathieson (Rangers)
4. John Greig, captain (Rangers)
5. Ron McKinnon (Rangers)
6. Jim Brogan (Celtic)
7. Tommy McLean (Kilmarnock)
8. Bobby Murdoch (Celtic)
9. Colin Stein (Rangers)
10. Willie Wallace (Celtic)
11. Peter Cormack (Hibernian)

■ A decent crowd of 17,657 turned up for the Scottish League v English League international of March 1971. Scotland, disappointingly, lost 1-0 to an early goal from Burnley's (soon to be Tottenham's) Ralph Coates.

■ Team v England, March 17, 1971:
1. Bobby Clark (Aberdeen)
2. Davie Hay (Celtic)
3. Billy Dickson (Kilmarnock)
4. Tom Forsyth (Motherwell)
   Sub, 64 min. George Connelly (Celtic)
5. Ron McKinnon, captain (Rangers)
6. Jim Brogan (Celtic)
7. Tommy McLean (Kilmarnock)
8. Tommy Callaghan (Celtic)
9. Davie Robb (Aberdeen)
10. Drew Jarvie (Airdrieonians)
11. Donald Ford (Hearts)

■ Hampden 1976. Leeds United's Trevor Cherry scores the only goal of what would turn out to be the last ever Scottish League v. English League game, in front of a crowd of 8,874.

■ Scottish League, March 17th, 1976.
1. Jim Stewart (Kilmarnock)
2. Andy Rolland (Dundee United)
   Sub, 84 min. John Greig (Rangers)
3. Joe Wark (Motherwell)
4. Colin Jackson, captain (Rangers)
5. Tom Forsyth (Rangers)
6. Alex MacDonald (Rangers)
7. Des Bremner (Hibernian)
8. Willie Miller (Aberdeen)
9. Joe Craig (Partick Thistle)
   Sub, 12 min. Peter Dickson (Queen of the South)
10. Bobby McKean (Rangers)
11. Arthur Duncan (Hibernian)

The 1970s. The best bad times

WE are Scottish. We like football. No, that doesn't quite capture it. We love football with a jealous, unreasonable intensity. It is an illness, and there is no cure. We don't want a cure. We are a nation obsessed.

We had, for many decades, the biggest football stadium in the world, despite being far from the biggest country in the world.

We measure ourselves as a nation by our football team's performance. We judge a man's manliness not just by his ability to play football but by the level of his devotion to the game.

We talk about football. We argue about football. We fight over football. We take incredible joy from wins, and suffer abject depression from defeats.

We laud football heroes as gods who walk among us, and revile failures as pariahs. The odour of a bad game, a missed penalty, an error at a crucial time, will hang around a man for the rest of his life.

The 1970s are remembered for their crushing disappointments. Scotland went to two World Cups and for greatly different reasons disappointed badly at both.

And there were some terrible results. Wembley 1975 was a truly awful, scarring, depressing experience. The February 1973 SFA "centenary celebration" against England was even worse, and a very cold night to boot!

But the 1970s are also remembered for the way we believed in ourselves. We regarded our team as one of the world's elite.

There were some fantastic results. We had possibly the two headiest nights in Scotland's football history, September 26th 1973, and October 12th 1977 (see pages 258 and 310).

When you take a long-term view of the whole experience of being a Scotland supporter, the 1970s was the best period we ever lived through. It was when wildly unreasonable ambitions became the norm.

There were points when we truly expected to beat any team we played. Anything seemed possible.

So carried away with self-belief did we get that it became a genuine surprise to lose against World Cup-winning nations, whose teams contained players who were among the greatest who ever took to a field.

There will probably never again be a decade when we feel this way. And that is sad. We felt we could take them all on, outplay them, out-score them, and out-drink them. It was inspiring, electrifying, intoxicating stuff. And we did it wearing flares.

Here's tae us? Wha's like us? Where is the coward that would not fight for such a land as Scotland – the birthplace of valour, the country of worth.

We flew so high we could have put out our hands and touched the face of God.

224

THE 1970s started with a flurry of very few goals.

Scotland's first three games of the decade were the Home Internationals, consisting of a 1-0 win in Northern Ireland (see page 228), then 0-0 draws with Wales and England at Hampden. But it isn't a lack of goals that the 1970 Scotland v. England match is remembered for.

■ **Left: Colin Stein nearly scores, but doesn't, against England.**

■ **Right: Ron McKinnon and Jimmy Johnstone match this by also not scoring.**

■ **Team v England, April 25th, 1970:**
1. **Jim Cruickshank (Hearts)**
2. **Tommy Gemmell (Celtic)**
3. **Billy Dickson (Kilmarnock)**
4. **John Greig, captain (Rangers)**
5. **Ron McKinnon (Rangers)**
6. **Bobby Moncur (Newcastle United)**
   Sub, 82 mins: Alan Gilzean (Tottenham Hotspur)
7. **Jimmy Johnstone (Celtic)**
8. **Davie Hay (Celtic)**
9. **Colin Stein (Rangers)**
10. **John O'Hare (Derby County)**
11. **Willie Carr (Coventry City)**

226

PENALTY REF, SURELY!

The Scotland-England game of 1970 is renowned for one of the worst refereeing decisions of all time.

In the 19th minute Everton centre-half Brian Labone mistimed a tackle on Colin Stein in the England box. He didn't get a touch on the ball, and sent Stein crashing to the turf.

It was as clear a penalty (left) as you'll see. But West German ref Gerhard Schulenberg didn't give it and the game finished 0-0.

Schulenberg was the ref who booked Derby County's Archie Gemmill and Roy McFarland for barely discernible offences in the first leg of The Rams' 1973 European Cup semi-final against Juventus, meaning the team's two most influential players were suspended for the second leg.

To this day Derby supporters mutter dark accusations.

■ **Right: Schulenberg did, however, give a foul for this grievous assault by Willie Carr on Nobby Stiles.**

IT was a year of odd refereeing decisions.

The Home International against Northern Ireland on a quagmire pitch at Windsor Park gave a moment of levity in what wasn't really a great game.

Georgie Best thought he should have had a penalty after a challenge from Ron McKinnon. But the English ref gave a foul against Best.

The somewhat unchuffed Manchester United superstar threw a handful of mud at McKinnon, who ducked, allowing the muck to hit the ref – who sent Best off!

■ **Team v Northern Ireland, April 18th, 1970:**
1. Bobby Clark (Aberdeen)
2. Davie Hay (Celtic)
3. Billy Dickson (Kilmarnock)
4. Frank McLintock, captain (Arsenal)
5. Ron McKinnon (Rangers)
6. Bobby Moncur (Newcastle United)
7. Tommy McLean (Kilmarnock)
8. Willie Carr (Coventry City)
9. John O'Hare (Derby County)
10. Alan Gilzean (Tottenham Hotspur)
    Sub: 70 min. Colin Stein (Rangers)
11. Willie Johnston (Rangers)

THERE are times when an international team has a bad patch. Indeed every football team that ever existed has games where it just doesn't work.

When it happens to Scotland there is withering fire from the sidelines. Newspapers are scathing in their condemnation of manager and players.

Some journalists are lenient when a club has a bad run. They don't want to lose sales among readers who are passionate supporters and can brook no criticism of the club no matter what results it is achieving on the park.

There are no constraints when it comes to the national team. The most savage football reports you will ever see in Scotland come when 11 men in dark blue have a bad game.

And so it was in 1971. And that's when managers are likely to be sacked.

■ Left: George Best shows how the game should be played as Northern Ireland win 1-0 at Hampden.

■ Team v. Northern Ireland, May 18th, 1971:
1. **Bobby Clark (Aberdeen)**
2. **Davie Hay (Celtic)**
3. **Jim Brogan (Celtic)**
4. **John Greig (Rangers)**
5. **Frank McLintock (Arsenal)**
   Sub, 71 min. Frank Munro (Wolverhampton Wanderers)
6. **Bobby Moncur, captain (Newcastle United)**
7. **Peter Lorimer (Leeds United)**
8. **Tony Green (Blackpool)**
9. **Eddie Gray (Leeds United)**
10. **Hugh Curran (Wolverhampton Wanderers)**
11. **John O'Hare (Derby County)**
    Sub, 46 min. Drew Jarvie (Airdrieonians)

■ Aberdeen's Davie Robb at the shallow end of Ninian Park in the 0-0 draw with Wales on what, even by 1970s standards, was regarded as a heavy pitch.

The difference in the quality of surface that used to be played on, compared to the billiard tables of the 21st Century, is one of the main differences between yesterday's and today's football.

■ Team v Wales, May 15th, 1971:
1. Bobby Clark (Aberdeen)
2. Davie Hay (Celtic)
3. Jim Brogan (Celtic)
4. Billy Bremner (Leeds United)
   Sub, 72 min. John Greig (Rangers)
5. Frank McLintock (Arsenal)
6. Bobby Moncur, captain (Newcastle United)
7. Peter Lorimer (Leeds United)
8. Peter Cormack (Nottingham Forest)
9. Eddie Gray (Leeds United)
10. Davie Robb (Aberdeen)
11. John O'Hare (Derby County)

WEMBLEY 1971 wasn't one of Scotland's more enjoyable visits to London. It was a match of tough tackles that we lost 3-1, seeing us finish bottom of the year's Home Internationals table with one point from the three games.

■ **Above: John Greig chases England's Franny Lee.**

■ **Right: As usual, the English (Leeds' Terry Cooper in this case) saved their most savage treatment for the unguarded shins of Jimmy Johnstone.**

■ **Team v England, May 22nd, 1971:**
1. Bobby Clark (Aberdeen)
2. John Greig (Rangers)
3. Jim Brogan (Celtic)
4. Billy Bremner (Leeds United)
5. Frank McLintock (Arsenal)
6. Bobby Moncur, captain (Newcastle United)
7. Jimmy Johnstone (Celtic)
8. Tony Green (Blackpool)
   Sub, 82 min. Drew Jarvie (Airdrieonians)
9. Peter Cormack (Nottingham Forest)
10. Davie Robb (Aberdeen)
11. Hugh Curran (Wolves)
   Sub, 46 min. Frank Munro (Wolverhampton Wanderers).

Doc's prescription

BOBBY BROWN was relieved of his post in the summer of 1971 (see page 346) and the charismatic Tommy Docherty took over, initially as caretaker.

As often happens in international football, a new boss meant a very different team. Tommy brought fresh ideas, renewed hope, and Anglos we'd previously barely heard of.

There were two meaningless European Championships 1972 qualifiers left in 1971, we had already lost away to Belgium and Denmark. The Doc took the return Belgium game to Pittodrie for a change of scenery (and was rewarded with a 36,500 crowd), where he threw on a youngster named Dalglish early in the second half.

Suddenly, Scotland were exciting again.

■ **Left: Bobby Clark gets up to punch clear on his Pittodrie home turf. The Scots won 1-0.**

■ **Right: Portuguese superstar Eusebio, with debutant Bob Wilson and a young Sandy Jardine behind, at Hampden in October 1971. The Scots won 2-1 with an excellent display of attacking football that effectively clinched the job for Docherty.**

■ **Team v Portugal, October 13th, 1971:**
1. Bob Wilson (Arsenal)
2. Sandy Jardine (Rangers)
3. Davie Hay (Celtic)
4. Pat Stanton (Hibernian)
5. Eddie Colquhoun (Sheffield United)
   Sub, 60 min. Martin Buchan (Aberdeen)
6. Jimmy Johnstone (Celtic)
7. Billy Bremner, captain (Leeds United)
8. George Graham (Arsenal)
9. Alex Cropley (Hibernian)
10. Archie Gemmill (Derby County)
11. John O'Hare (Derby County)

■ **Team v Belgium, November 10th, 1971:**
1. Bobby Clark (Aberdeen)
2. Sandy Jardine (Rangers)
3. Davie Hay (Celtic)
4. Pat Stanton (Hibernian)
5. Martin Buchan (Aberdeen)
6. Jimmy Johnstone (Celtic)
   Sub, 79 min. John Hansen (Partick Thistle)
7. Billy Bremner, captain (Leeds United)
8. Alex Cropley (Hibernian)
   Sub, 48 min. Kenny Dalglish (Celtic)
9. Eddie Gray (Leeds United)
10. Steve Murray (Aberdeen)
11. John O'Hare (Derby County)

The return of the The King. After a three-year absence, mainly due to injuries, Denis Law – the King of Old Trafford – was back in a Scotland jersey and had the honour of captaining the team in a friendly against Peru. In a tough game against a well-organised defence, he scored the second in a 2-0 win.

■ **Above: This early chance didn't go in, but Denis pulled down a pass from O'Hare in the second half and lashed the ball into the roof of the net.**

■ **Right: Denis swaps pennants with Peru captain Hector Chumpitaz.**

■ Team v Peru, April 26th, 1972:
1. Ally Hunter (Kilmarnock)
2. John Brownlie (Hibernian)
3. Willie Donachie (Manchester City)
4. Bobby Moncur (Newcastle United)
5. Eddie Colquhoun (Sheffield United)
6. Willie Morgan (Manchester United)
7. Willie Carr (Coventry City)
8. Asa Hartford (West Bromwich Albion)
9. John O'Hare (Derby County)
10. Denis Law, captain (Manchester United)
11. Archie Gemmill (Derby County)

BY early 1972 the good feeling was still growing. Scotland had excellent players drawn from club sides used to winning. The line-ups below contain some of our all-time-great names.

Pangs of confidence were felt.

■ **Left: Peter Lorimer v Wales.**

■ **Right: Jimmy Johnstone v Northern Ireland.**

■ **Team v Northern Ireland, May 20th, 1972:**
1. Bobby Clark (Aberdeen)
2. John Brownlie (Hibernian)
3. Willie Donachie (Manchester City)
4. Billy Bremner, captain (Leeds United)
5. Billy McNeill (Celtic)
6. Bobby Moncur (Newcastle United)
7. Jimmy Johnstone (Celtic)
   Sub. 61 min. Peter Lorimer (Leeds United)
8. Archie Gemmill (Derby County)
9. John O'Hare (Derby County)
10. Denis Law (Manchester United)
11. George Graham (Arsenal)

■ **Team v Wales, May 24th, 1972:**
1. Bobby Clark (Aberdeen)
2. Martin Buchan (Manchester United)
3. Pat Stanton (Hibernian)
4. Billy Bremner, captain (Leeds United)
5. Billy McNeill (Celtic)
6. Bobby Moncur (Newcastle United)
7. Peter Lorimer (Leeds United)
8. Archie Gemmill (Derby County)
   Sub, 35 min. Asa Hartford (West Bromwich Albion)
9. John O'Hare (Derby County)
   Sub, 56 min. Lou Macari (Celtic)
10. Denis Law (Manchester United)
11. Tony Green (Newcastle United)

239

A blip against England in 1972. We went down 1-0 at Hampden to an Alan Ball goal.

There were a few rumblings in the Scottish press about "too many Anglos". And this was another bad-tempered clash with the English, a game that saw 46 fouls committed.

But it is always difficult to beat a nation that has many times our population, and so has many more players to choose from. It is amazing that we have triumphed over them so often over so many years.

Scotland's population is roughly similar to Finland, who have played England 11 times in their history but never once beaten them.

■ **Team v England, May 27th, 1972:**
1. Bobby Clark (Aberdeen)
2. John Brownlie (Hibernian)
3. Willie Donachie (Manchester City)
   Sub, 74 min. Tony Green (Newcastle United)
4. Bobby Moncur (Newcastle United)
5. Billy McNeill (Celtic)
6. Peter Lorimer (Leeds United)
7. Billy Bremner, captain (Leeds United)
8. Archie Gemmill (Derby County)
   Sub, 49 min. Jimmy Johnstone (Celtic)
9. Asa Hartford (West Bromwich Albion)
10. Lou Macari (Celtic)
11. Denis Law (Manchester United)

Prince Kenny

KENNY DALGLISH announced himself as a first-pick Scotland player in November 1972, with a goal after two minutes (pictured left) of our World Cup Qualifier against Denmark. We played the away fixture the previous month and turned in another good display to win 4-1.

The Danish goal was scored by Finn Laudrup, father of Michael and Brian.

These wins lit the fires beneath Scotland's World Cup 1974 quest. It all seemed to be going well . . .

■ **Team v Denmark, October 18th, 1972:**
1. Bobby Clark (Aberdeen)
2. John Brownlie (Hibernian)
3. Alex Forsyth (Partick Thistle)
4. Martin Buchan (Manchester United)
5. Eddie Colquhoun (Sheffield United)
6. Billy Bremner, captain (Leeds United)
7. Peter Lorimer (Leeds United)
8. George Graham (Arsenal)
9. Willie Morgan (Manchester United)
10. Lou Macari (Celtic)
    Sub, 88 min. Kenny Dalglish (Celtic)
11. Jimmy Bone (Norwich City)
    Sub, 65 min. Joe Harper (Aberdeen)

■ **Team v Denmark, November 15th, 1972:**
1. David Harvey (Leeds United)
2. John Brownlie (Hibernian)
3. Willie Donachie (Manchester City)
4. Billy Bremner, captain (Leeds United)
5. Martin Buchan (Manchester United)
6. Eddie Colquhoun (Sheffield United)
7. Peter Lorimer (Leeds United)
8. Kenny Dalglish (Celtic)
    Sub, 75 min. Willie Carr (Coventry City)
9. Joe Harper (Aberdeen)
10. George Graham (Arsenal)
11. Willie Morgan (Manchester United)

The Scottish rollercoaster ride

SCOTLAND'S international football history is a rollercoaster ride. It always has been, it probably always will be.

The national side almost never trundles along on the level. It is either up (and everything is wonderful, a glittering future lies ahead). Or it is down (in the deepest depths, there can be no way out of this nightmare). If you aren't used to this by now, just where have you been?

By late 1972, we were looking good for qualification for the World Cup of 1974 and the Scottish Football Association was about to celebrate its centenary year with glamour matches against England, Brazil and West Germany.

Then Manchester United waved their chequebook at our confident, charismatic, successful manager Tommy Docherty. Off he went.

A new man was needed and, eventually, the job went to former Famous Five star Willie Ormond (see page 350) who had been quietly building a St Johnstone side that looked like it could really start to challenge for major honours.

Willie's reign started terribly.

Sir Alf Ramsey's England came to Hampden on an icy February night to "celebrate" the SFA's first 100 years and handed out a football lesson.

It was ugly. A terrible display on a frozen pitch and one of our lowest ever points. It became known as the St Valentine's Day Massacre.

England won 5-0 in front of an angry 48,470 crowd who, far from "Bonnie Scotland, we'll support you ever more" sang only about their desire to have their ticket money refunded and lit bonfires on the Hampden terraces.

Willie Ormond was a very different, a much more quietly thoughtful, man to Tommy Docherty. But he was visibly angry with his players that night.

Several would never play for Scotland again.

■ **Right: A rare photo of a Scotland attack in the centenary humbling. The ball's resemblance to a solar eclipse is a result of primitive 1970s photo editing.**

■ **Team v England, February 14th, 1973:**
1. **Bobby Clark (Aberdeen)**
2. **Alex Forsyth (Manchester United)**
3. **Willie Donachie (Manchester City)**
4. **Martin Buchan (Manchester United)**
5. **Eddie Colquhoun (Sheffield United)**
6. **Peter Lorimer (Leeds United)**
7. **Billy Bremner, captain (Leeds United)**
8. **George Graham (Manchester United)**
9. **Willie Morgan (Manchester United)**
    Sub, 19 mins. Colin Stein (Coventry City)
10. **Lou Macari (Manchester United)**
11. **Kenny Dalglish (Celtic)**

Don't mention the war

SCOTLAND versus England matches had been becoming ever tougher, and dirtier, encounters for several years by this point – which reflects the way the game was changing in the late 1960s and early '70s.

Every club side of that era had hard men. The exploits of such names as Norman "bites yer legs" Hunter, Ron "Chopper" Harris, Tommy Smith, Billy Bremner, and Kenny Burns have passed down through the years and have become legend.

You'll find many an older supporter who misses the days of the granite-versus-iron, full-blooded 50-50 tackles. The days when it was a "man's game".

It was, indeed, almost a different sport to that which is played today.

The standard of refereeing in the early 1970s, however, remained gentlemanly – the referees were 20 years behind the times and would wave fingers or give a "ticking-off" while the tackles became ever more lethal.

Off the pitch, the problem of football hooliganism was reaching crisis point. Tens of thousands of Scots would still travel to Wembley for matches, but there were more and more frightening stories told of skinhead gangs roaming the streets of London looking for trouble on the Friday night before and Saturday night after the game.

However, those on the pitch wearing the dark blue had other problems. The terrible events of the St Valentine's Day Massacre were still fresh in the minds of fans, and journalists, and "pride in the shirt" was called for on the pages of newspapers and in many a shout from the terraces.

Scotland rose to the occasion and were unlucky to lose that game 1-0.

They had great chances to score themselves and one Shilton save from a Dalglish volley can only be termed "miraculous". Some national pride had been restored but, again – brave Scots go down fighting.

■ **Right: Peter Shilton gets to a high ball. This was the England keeper's breakthrough game, he would henceforth be seen as the natural successor to Gordon Banks.**

■ **Team v England, May 19th, 1973:**
1. **Ally Hunter (Celtic)**
2. **Sandy Jardine (Rangers)**
3. **Danny McGrain (Celtic)**
4. **Billy Bremner, captain (Leeds United)**
5. **Jim Holton (Manchester United)**
6. **Derek Johnstone (Rangers)**
7. **Willie Morgan (Manchester United)**
8. **Lou Macari (Manchester United)**
   Sub, 74 min. Joe Jordan (Leeds United)
9. **Kenny Dalglish (Celtic)**
10. **Davie Hay (Celtic)**
11. **Peter Lorimer (Leeds United)**
    Sub, 80 min. Colin Stein (Coventry City)

248

■ Two more shots from Wembley 1973. Left, Scotland keeper Ally Hunter punches clear.
■ Above: Big Jim Holton (six foot two, eyes of blue) gets the man he is after, England striker Allan Clarke.

THE second instalment of the SFA centenary trilogy was another visit by the charismatic Brazil side.

Everyone in Scotland expected an exhibition of flicks, tricks, and all the flair the South Americans were famous for. Instead they were treated to a bad-tempered, tough-tackling match that ended 1-0 in favour of those in yellow shirts, due to a highly unfortunate Derek Johnstone own-goal.

In an early sponsorship venture, Adidas delivered a large supply of boots to Hampden and paid every Scot who wore them £75 – about £950 today, adjusted for inflation.

■ **Team v Brazil, June 30th, 1973:**
1. Peter McCloy (Rangers)
2. Sandy Jardine (Rangers)
3. Danny McGrain (Celtic)
4. Billy Bremner, captain (Leeds United)
5. Jim Holton (Manchester United)
6. Derek Johnstone (Rangers)
7. Willie Morgan (Manchester United)
8. Davie Hay (Celtic)
9. Derek Parlane (Rangers)
10. Joe Jordan (Leeds United)
11. Kenny Dalglish (Celtic)
    Sub, 70 min. George Graham (Manchester United)

■ A close thing for the Brazilians.

■ **Danny McGrain bemused at the Brazilians' moaning and complaining, as English referee Ken Burns attempts to keep the peace between Rivelino and Joe Jordan.**

■ Derek Parlane puts in a challenge. The Brazilian defender is clearly indlulging in what would (in later years) become known as "simulation". Back then, when speech was plainer, we called it a dive.

Barbed wire Billy

PINNED above his peg in Leeds United's Elland Road dressing room, Billy Bremner kept a sign that simply said: "Keep Fighting".

Highly respected English writer and sports commentator John Arlott said of Billy in the late 1960s: "Above all, Leeds have Bremner, the best footballer in the four countries. If every manager in Britain were given his choice of any one player to add to his team some, no doubt, would toy with the idea of George Best. But the realists, to a man, would have Bremner."

Possibly the best reference to him is a description they give in Yorkshire: "Billy was 10-and-a-half stone of barbed wire."

He was perhaps the greatest Scotland captain of them all. His will to win is the stuff of legend. He'd do anything, run any distance, tackle any giant, to win.

He was the epitome of the famous Scottish fighting spirit. The sort of man that you'd want on your side in the trenches. The sort of player you'd put in your team even if he was injured because he affected those around him. He played around 60 games a season for club and country for five seasons in a row. An almost indestructible man.

It is almost quarter of a century since Billy died at the tragically young age of 54 and a statue of him now stands outside the Elland Road stadium.

To this day, Leeds United supporters hold a quote by Billy close to their heart. It is just five words and is carved on the plinth of his statue. It is how they want the ethos of their club to be seen. The words are: "Side before self, every time".

The seeds of the Tartan Army

SCOTLAND hadn't taken part in a World Cup Finals tournament for 16 long years when the qualifying groups for West Germany 1974 reached their climax.

In that space of time, the World Cup had grown to be regarded as the pinnacle of the game, rather than the foreign sideshow that the inward-looking home nations had treated it as in the 1950s.

England winning in 1966 had opened our eyes to the enormity of it all, and the razzmatazz surrounding Mexico '70, with its storied Brazil side, had been another giant leap for the world game.

We were desperate to play our part in what had become, and still is, the biggest sporting occasion on the planet.

Only 16 teams were to go to the '74 finals. Qualification was heavily weighted towards European nations at that time. Nine would make it through, along with four from South America, one African, one Asian/Oceania, and one North American.

By the autumn of 1973, Scotland's task was clear. The other teams in our three-nation group were Denmark and Czechoslovakia. We'd beaten Denmark home and away, and then – crucially – the Danes had held the Czechs 1-1 in Copenhagen.

So we had a double-header with Czechoslovakia, but knew we needed just a win against them in the first game at Hampden to clinch qualification and leave the away game as a dead rubber.

Wednesday, September the 26th, 1973, was the crunch night. It was a sell-out 100,000 crowd and the first time that a Scotland home game other than a Home International had been shown live on TV.

It is no exaggeration to say the entire nation was watching.

We started well, physically giving as good as we got in a couple of bruising encounters with the tall and strong Eastern Europeans.

But then disaster struck.

On 33 minutes Dukla Prague winger Zdenek Nehoda tried a speculative shot from well outside the box, but so far over to the flank that it might have been a cross. It was about waist-high and not particularly hard – but somehow it went through Ally Hunter's hands and into the net.

Hampden was momentarily silenced.

Football crowds are a capricious lot. Sometimes the loss of a goal kills an atmosphere stone dead for the rest of the game. At other times it galvanises ever more fervent support.

The chants quickly started up again and were delivered even more enthusiastically, fuelled by what was obviously becoming a supreme effort from the lads on the pitch.

Soon the support was even louder than it had been before the goal.

It was a night that would make the hairs on any Scotsman's neck stand on end. The noise was incredible, it was one of those games where the crowd seems to act as one entity and with one voice.

Scotland went on to score two goals amid dramatic scenes (see the next couple of pages).

While this would be a memorable night for the players, it is also remembered for the great performance, indeed one of the best in history, by the Hampden crowd.

Scotland's matches before this had sometimes had an uneasy atmosphere. There were many occasions when club chants had been sung. It wasn't unusual to hear cheers for players from one half of the Old Firm, and jeers for those from the other side – no matter if they had been playing well or not.

Players attached to English clubs were (as is discussed earlier in this book) also much more likely to get stick from the crowd, and would even be booed.

After defeats, players would be apportioned blame depending on the club they were signed to rather than their actual performance in the game.

If there is one match that the end of this poor state of affairs can be traced to, then it is this one.

The Scotland support was unified during that game, all sides of the stadium urging on those in dark blue no matter which club team they played for, or which country that club was based in.

It was a fantastic night when all of Scotland spoke, and sang, as one.

All who recall it will tell of the endless "Bonnie Scotland, Bonnie Scotland, We'll support you ever more" chants that came from all parts of the ground – even from the cigar-smoking gentlemen wearing camel coats sitting in the South Stand!

This unity carried on down the years.

Despite what you might be told, or how it might look 50 or 60 years later, trips to Wembley were often far from a cheery day out for one big happy family. There were always club factions within the support and intimidation, even violence, wasn't unusual.

And the behaviour towards the locals when in London was often atrocious.

The Tartan Army as a distinct culture with its strict, self-policing manner of behaving well was still some way off. The charity-conscious activities, idiosyncratic song repertoire, and friendly traditions that make up the modern Tartan Army would be forged during away trips and World Cup jaunts over the coming years.

But the seeds of fan togetherness, when being a Scotland fan was the only qualification required, and the giving of consistent, cheerful support the default position, were sewn that heady night in 1973.

THIS wasn't an easy game by any means. Czechoslovakia were one of Europe's top sides in the early 1970s.

The nation had a formidable footballing history, having been beaten finalists in the 1934 and 1962 World Cups

They would go on to win the European Championships in 1976 with the famous Antonin Panenka chipped penalty (that for ever after bore his name) deciding the penalty shoot-out with the then world champions West Germany.

Panenka played that night at Hampden.

■ **Right: Jim Holton scored the equaliser just before half-time, making a prodigious leap to get up and nod home a Willie Morgan corner.**

■ Big Joe Jordan, partially hidden by the Czech keeper, places his glorious winning header just inside the post. What a night it was!

Wily Willie

WILLIE ORMOND, known to his players as Donny or sometimes the Big O, hadn't had the easiest of starts to his career as Scotland manager, but he got his tactics just right that night at Hampden.

He had consulted Sir Alf Ramsey, whose England team had played the Czechs in a friendly in May 1973. The secret was, Ormond reckoned, that though almost the entire Czech team were tall men, their central defenders were vulnerable. The big shy laddies didn't exactly attack crosses.

Ormond started with Kenny Dalglish and Denis Law as main strikers, both had been in great form for their club sides. But as the game wore on he threw on young Joe Jordan.

At the time, Joe was finding it difficult to dislodge Mick Jones from the Leeds United centre-forward berth, so this was a slightly surprising substitution. But, of course, Jordan was a natural header of a ball and at 21 was already an aggressive and powerful athlete.

He had only been on the pitch for 12 minutes when a superb ball from the outside of Willie Morgan's boot found him between the centre-halves and free to plant an unstoppable diving header past Ivo Viktor.

■ Team v Czechoslovakia, September 26th, 1973:
1. Ally Hunter (Celtic)
2. Sandy Jardine (Rangers)
3. Danny McGrain (Celtic)
4. Billy Bremner, captain (Leeds United)
5. Jim Holton (Manchester United)
6. George Connelly (Celtic)
7. Willie Morgan (Manchester United)
8. Davie Hay (Celtic)
9. Denis Law (Manchester City)
10. Kenny Dalglish (Celtic)
    Sub, 63 min. Joe Jordan (Leeds United)
11. Tommy Hutchison (Coventry City)

■ **Right: One of the all-time-great Scottish football photos. Joe celebrates that famous goal with Tommy Hutchison and Billy Bremner.**

The fine art of picking up scraps

DENIS LAW had been out of the Scotland picture for all of 1970 and 1971, and had again been out at the start of 1973 before being recalled for this game. He had undergone knee surgery and moved from Manchester United to Manchester City – to everyone's surprise as he had been widely tipped to take a coaching role at United.

But the fires still burned. Denis ran his heart out for 90 minutes, to the acclaim of the crowd.

Denis was always (as had been his trademark for years) ready to pounce on any tiny mistake made by the goalkeeper. As shown above, if he wasn't having a shot or header on goal himself he would rapidly follow up a team-mate's shot in case the ball came loose.

Experience is the key to this sort of anticipation. The trick was to read the game and react before a defender. Denis's inhumanly quick reactions greatly helped.

266

■As captain and man of the match, Billy Bremner was chaired round Hampden during the lap of honour. Billy then went to fetch Willie Ormond, who (Willie said after the game) had gone into the dressing room to allow his players to take the plaudits from the ecstatic crowd. Willie was also, he admitted years later, suffering a sore head, having bashed his skull against the dugout roof when Jordan's winner went in.

■ Team v Northern Ireland, May 11th, 1974:
1. David Harvey (Leeds United)
2. Sandy Jardine (Rangers)
3. Willie Donachie (Manchester City)
   Sub, 46 min. Jim Smith (Newcastle United)
4. Martin Buchan (Manchester United)
5. Jim Holton (Manchester United)
6. Tommy Hutchison (Coventry City)
7. Billy Bremner, captain (Leeds United)
8. Davie Hay (Celtic)
9. Willie Morgan (Manchester United)
10. Kenny Dalglish (Celtic)
11. Denis Law (Manchester City)
   Sub, 65 min. Joe Jordan (Leeds United)

■ Left: Denis Law always told defenders exactly what he thought of them and what he thought of their attempts at tackles. If they gave him verbals, he gave it back. If they went in hard (and most did in those days) Denis showed no mercy either. In this photo he is giving Northern Ireland defender Sammy Nelson (of Arsenal) a piece of his mind.

SCOTLAND qualified for the 1974 World Cup, but England, thanks to a fantastic display by Polish "clown" goalkeeper Jan Tomaszewski, didn't. Neither did either of the other home nations. So Scotland went into the 1974 Home Championships in buoyant mood as the UK's sole representatives on the world stage.

During the Home Championships the squad were invited – for refreshments – to a hotel close to the Queens Hotel Largs (the HQ for the week). On the way back Jimmy Johnstone took the buoyancy feeling to extremes, climbing into a rowing boat at about 5am in the morning. Sandy Jardine playfully gave the boat a wee shove away from the quayside with his foot.

To Jimmy's credit – while drifting down the Firth of Clyde, with no oars, and unable to swim – he comically sang several verses of "Michael row the boat ashore" to his team-mates. The rest of the lads had thought this a greatly funny jape to begin with, but began to worry for Jimmy's life as he disappeared out to sea.

The coastguards were hastily called. Jimmy the sailor man was rescued off the coast of Great Cumbrae and brought back, a shade of pale blue, shivering violently.

This was seized upon by commentators as proof of the modern footballer's drunken excesses. Willie Ormond "had a quiet word" with the squad, but didn't make too big a thing of it, and Scotland – with Jimmy in his place on the wing – beat England 2-0 a couple of days later.

The newspapers did make a big thing of it, though. Jimmy saluted the press box at the final whistle, appearing to suggest the reporters had been wrong on two counts.

■ **Right: Jimmy celebrates the win over England with Sandy Jardine and Joe Jordan.**

TO this day there is controversy over whether the first goal in Scotland's 1974 2-0 win over England at a packed Hampden Park should count as an OG by England's Stoke City full-back Mike Pejic (wearing No. 3 in this photo) or be chalked up next to Joe's name in the all-time Scotland goalscorers' tally.

You can easily find it online.

Let's lay this to rest once and for all: it was Joe's goal.

■ **Left: Joe watches his shot go into the net.**

■ **Team v England, May 18th, 1974:**
1. **David Harvey (Leeds United)**
2. **Sandy Jardine (Rangers)**
3. **Danny McGrain (Celtic)**
4. **Billy Bremner, captain (Leeds United)**
5. **Jim Holton (Manchester United)**
6. **John Blackley (Hibernian)**
7. **Jimmy Johnstone (Celtic)**
8. **Davie Hay (Celtic)**
9. **Joe Jordan (Leeds United)**
10. **Kenny Dalglish (Celtic)**
11. **Peter Lorimer (Leeds United)**

■ Celebrations in '74. It means a lot, to every Scot, to beat England. This is not to overblow it, nor should we fixate upon it. But it is important, it carries a lot of history. It is the oldest international in the world. And beating your neighbour – who is 10 times your size – deserves to be celebrated. It is why derbies are so special.

At time of writing, before the European Championships encounter of 2021, the match had been played 114 times. England had won 48, Scotland 41, and there had been 25 draws – only three were 0-0. Adjusted for population size, Scotland have massively over-performed in this fixture.

World Cup West Germany 1974

WE didn't win it, but this was a very different experience at a World Cup. Our 1954 and '58 ventures were pitiful, this one has the word "pride" stamped over its memory.

The word you hear whenever Scotland and West Germany 1974 are mentioned is "unlucky". And that is deserved. But, truly, the words that should be associated with that tournament are: brilliant, skilful, battling, and organised.

Even in a tournament that could boast Franz Beckenbauer's West Germany and Johann Cruyff's Netherlands, we were among the best teams on show.

And saying that isn't hyperbole, nor is it a conclusion made with dark blue-tinted glasses on. We were very good.

The only mistake was a decent, but not spectacular or adventurous, performance against Zaire. That was our downfall. A 2-0 win in that game (our first ever win at a World Cup finals tournament) turned out to not quite be enough.

It is only with the benefit of hindsight that people would say we should have pressed forward more, and scored more goals. The consensus immediately after the game was mostly that the Scots had played a professional, controlled game. Davie Hay hit the Zaire post, and Peter Lorimer hit the bar.

It was hailed as a "tournament performance", the sort of careful and efficient start that cup-winning teams might put in, saving their best for the bigger games.

We then outplayed, out-fought, and should have beaten the Brazilians. We had the best chance of the game, but it finished 0-0. Despite the awe that was given to the Brazilian players of that era, Billy Bremner was the best man on the park.

In the last game we were every bit as good as the Yugoslav side that many pundits had tipped to be at least semi-finalists.

We gave ourselves a mountain to climb after losing the first goal, but for once did actually manage to climb the mountain. The Yugoslavs had a formidable, and deserved, reputation for possessing a well-drilled defence. But we equalised, albeit very late, through a Joe Jordan header.

The last few minutes of that 1-1 draw were the cruellest in Scottish football history.

Playing in Frankfurt, we thought we'd qualified as the latest word from the Brazil-Zaire game in Gelsenkirchen was that the South Americans were winning only 2-0. This meant we would go through. We'd have four points, the same as Brazil and Yugoslavia – but we'd scored one more goal as the Brazilians had drawn 0-0 with us and 0-0 with Yugoslavia.

When news came through that winger Valdomiro had scored a late third for Brazil, we were devastated to be out of the competition. The first nation to ever go home from a World Cup without losing a game, and having conceded just one goal in three games.

Brazil scored a solitary goal more against Zaire than we did. One goal. That was the margin that put us out.

It was the hardest hard luck story in Scotland's hard-won collection of hard luck stories. Brave Scots go down fighting. Yet again.

The Scottish public greeted the squad as heroes. They flew home to a tartan scarf-bedecked 10,000 crowd at Glasgow Airport and lining the streets outside. Willie Ormond and the boys were swamped by supporters singing "We'll support you ever more" as they got off the plane.

One can only imagine the scenes that might have taken place if we'd got further in the competition.

These were good times.

Indeed you could argue that this was the high point of Scottish international football history to date. The time when we were so good that it was genuinely a surprise to not qualify from a World Cup group that contained the reigning world champions and the finalists of the 1968 European Championships.

■ **Right: Joe Jordan tangles with the Zaire defence.**

THOUGH Scotland went out of that World Cup because they didn't score enough goals against Zaire, it wasn't really the game against the Africans that was the problem – it was the game against Brazil.

That was the missed opportunity.

The fabled yellow shirts seemed to have abandoned the free-flowing football of four years earlier and decided that as everyone tried to kick them, they'd do some kicking back. We should have heeded their brutal performance at Hampden a year earlier.

Billy Bremner seemed to be the main target, taking several ridiculous tackles from Rivelino.

Hacking competitions were part of the game in the 1970s and we had men who were often involved in very tough encounters, yet could still play to their potential. If anyone could handle a bit of aggro (as it was called back then) then it was Billy.

We could have, and should have, beaten that Brazil team.

Scotland played their first game in Borussia Dortmund's Westfalenstadion, the final two in Eintracht Frankfurt's Waldstadion.

The shirt numbers in the teams on the right aren't the actual numbers worn, the team numbers are given in an attempt to show (roughly) the formation that was played. The players had squad numbers (see below) for the tournament.

The full squad was:

Goalkeepers: 1. David Harvey (Leeds United), 12. Thomson Allan (Dundee), 13. Jim Stewart (Kilmarnock).

Defenders: 2. Sandy Jardine (Rangers), 3. Danny McGrain (Celtic), 5. Jim Holton (Manchester United), 6. John Blackley (Hibernian), 14. Martin Buchan (Manchester United), 16. Willie Donachie (Manchester City), 21. Gordon McQueen (Leeds United), 22. Erich Schaedler (Hibernian).

Midfielders: 4. Billy Bremner, captain (Leeds United), 7. Jimmy Johnstone (Celtic), 10. Davie Hay (Celtic), 15. Peter Cormack (Liverpool), 17. Donald Ford (Hearts), 18. Tommy Hutchison (Coventry City).

Forwards: 8. Kenny Dalglish (Celtic), 9. Joe Jordan (Leeds United), 11. Peter Lorimer (Leeds United), 19. Denis Law (Manchester City), 20. Willie Morgan (Manchester United).

■ Team v Zaire, June 14th, 1974:
1. David Harvey (Leeds United)
2. Sandy Jardine (Rangers)
3. Danny McGrain (Celtic)
4. John Blackley (Hibernian)
5. Jim Holton (Manchester United)
6. Peter Lorimer (Leeds United)
7. Billy Bremner, captain (Leeds United)
8. Davie Hay (Celtic)
9. Joe Jordan (Leeds United)
10. Kenny Dalglish (Celtic)
   Sub, 75 min. Tommy Hutchison (Coventry City)
11. Denis Law (Manchester City)

■ Team v Brazil, June 18th, 1974:
1. David Harvey (Leeds United)
2. Sandy Jardine (Rangers)
3. Danny McGrain (Celtic)
4. Martin Buchan (Manchester United)
5. Jim Holton (Manchester United)
6. Peter Lorimer (Leeds United)
7. Billy Bremner (Leeds United)
8. Davie Hay (Celtic)
9. Joe Jordan (Leeds United)
10. Kenny Dalglish (Celtic)
11. Willie Morgan (Manchester United)

■ Team v Yugoslavia, June 22nd, 1974:
1. David Harvey (Leeds United)
2. Sandy Jardine (Rangers)
3. Danny McGrain (Celtic)
4. Martin Buchan (Manchester United)
5. Jim Holton (Manchester United)
6. Peter Lorimer (Leeds United)
7. Billy Bremner (Leeds United)
8. Davie Hay (Celtic)
9. Joe Jordan (Leeds United)
10. Kenny Dalglish (Celtic)
   Sub, 65 min. Tommy Hutchison (Coventry City)
11. Willie Morgan (Manchester United)

Willie Ormond tried to put Jimmy Johnstone on as a late sub in the Yugoslavia game, but neither he nor the linesman could attract the Mexican referee's attention.

New heroes

As always happens after big international tournaments, there is a changing of the guard. Old faces disappear, the baton is handed on to a new generation.

You'll have had to turn your book on its side again to look at this photo of Leeds centre-half Gordon McQueen, seen here comprehensively outjumping Wales' John Toshack in the 1975 Home International. Gordon would be a giant of the Scottish international side for years to come.

OTHER players who would make their debut around this time and go on to make their mark for Scotland include Bruce Rioch, Willie Miller, and Graeme Souness.

■ **Right: Rioch (extreme left) scores a free-kick against Denmark in 1975**

■ **Team v Wales, May 17th, 1975:**
1. Stewart Kennedy (Rangers)
2. Sandy Jardine, captain (Rangers)
3. Danny McGrain, (Celtic)
4. Colin Jackson (Rangers)
   Sub, 77 min. Frank Munro (Wolverhampton Wanderers)
5. Gordon McQueen (Leeds United)
6. Bruce Rioch (Derby County)
7. Lou Macari (Manchester United)
8. Arthur Duncan (Hibernian)
9. Derek Parlane (Rangers)
10. Kenny Dalglish (Celtic)
11. Ted MacDougall (Norwich City)

■ **Team v Denmark, October 29th, 1975:**
1. David Harvey (Leeds United)
2. Danny McGrain (Celtic)
3. Stewart Houston (Manchester United)
4. John Greig, captain (Rangers)
5. Colin Jackson (Rangers)
6. Peter Lorimer (Leeds United)
7. Asa Hartford (Manchester City)
8. Bruce Rioch (Derby County)
9. Archie Gemmill (Derby County)
10. Kenny Dalglish (Celtic)
11. Ted MacDougall (Norwich City)
    Sub, 85 min. Derek Parlane (Rangers)

THERE'S not much good to recall about Wembley 1975. Scotland lost 5-1. But one thing has to be said: goalkeeper Stewart Kennedy didn't deserve all the blame.

Of the five goals, none were blatantly goalkeeping errors. The fourth was a deflection. Kennedy made a fantastic save for the fifth and should have been able to expect a defender to be in among the three Englishmen lining up to put away the rebound from the bar.

Kennedy's only real mistake was that he didn't use the old goalkeeping trick of flamboyant dives when shots went past him that he couldn't possibly have reached. Staying static made him look bad. But no amount of pretend dives would have made any difference to the goals going in.

As for the performance itself, Scotland weren't good by any means, but they weren't that bad either. England had outstanding performances from Kevin Keegan, Alan Ball, and Gerry Francis – three men who were, when on-song, among the best players in Europe at the time.

Scotland badly missed the six Leeds United players who were the team's backbone. Leeds were to play Bayern Munich (and be horribly cheated) in the European Cup Final four days later.

■ Team v England, May 24th 13th, 1975:
1. Stewart Kennedy (Rangers)
2. Sanday Jardine, captain (Rangers)
3. Danny McGrain (Celtic)
4. Frank Munro (Wolverhampton Wanderers)
5. Gordon McQueen (Leeds United)
6. Alfie Conn (Tottenham)
7. Bruce Rioch (Derby County)
8. Kenny Dalglish (Celtic)
9. Derek Parlane (Rangers)
10. Ted MacDougall (Norwich City)
    Sub, 71 min. Lou Macari (Manchester United)
11. Arthur Duncan (Hibernian)
    Sub 61 min. Tommy Hutchison (Coventry City)

■ The deflected fourth goes in off Kennedy's left-hand post.

From way up high to way down low

SCOTLAND don't really "do" middle-of-the-road. They are up or they are down. Motoring on to greatness, or suffering a car crash.

The good feeling around the national team following the 1974 World Cup quickly blew away, like the cigarette smoke you used to see above the Hampden crowd as everyone lit up at half-time.

Within a year we had failed to qualify for the Euro Championships of 1976. This was the last year that the Euros finals would consist of four teams, it became eight, then 16, and is now a 24-team tournament.

We also suffered the "Copenhagen Incident", which resulted in five players being given life bans.

There are several accounts of what happened.

Shenanigans went on, there is no doubt of that. The players had permission to go out but were drinking from duty-free bottles as Danish bar prices were so high. There was trouble at a nightclub, resulting in several Scots being thrown out of the place. But no one was arrested, no complaints were made to police.

There also seems to have been a fist fight back at the hotel, possibly Billy Bremner against a member of the SFA – accounts vary. It is probably true that a lot of things went on. But with so much drink taken it became difficult to unravel who did what to whom, when, where and why.

The upshot was that Bremner, Willie Young, Joe Harper, Arthur Graham and Pat McCluskey were banned for life, without even being allowed in to speak up for themselves at the SFA committee meeting where the decision was made.

The sentences were fairly quickly lifted, not least because several of the players who were banned had nothing whatsoever to do with it all. But Bremner, aged 34, never played for Scotland again.

By the time Scotland played Romania in the dead rubber at the end of the Euros qualifying group, several new faces were around.

With the terrible loss to England, the Euros failure, and the Copenhagen incident, it seemed Willie Ormond's coat was on a shoogly peg.

■ **Scotland v Romania, December 17th, 1975:**
1. **Jim Cruickshank (Hearts)**
2. **John Brownlie (Hibernian)**
3. **Willie Donachie (Manchester City)**
4. **Martin Buchan, captain (Manchester United)**
5. **Colin Jackson (Rangers)**
6. **Bruce Rioch (Derby County)**
7. **Kenny Dalglish (Celtic)**
   Sub, 73 min. Ted MacDougall (Norwich City)
8. **Johnny Doyle (Ayr United)**
   Sub, 73 min. Peter Lorimer (Leeds United)
9. **Andy Gray (Aston Villa)**
10. **Asa Hartford (Manchester City)**
11. **Archie Gemmill (Derby County)**

■ **Right: Andy Gray making his debut v Romania.**

The in-form man

IT is one of the great selection problems for any Scotland manager. Pick the striker on a blistering run of domestic form, but with little international experience? Or pick the tried and tested man who has been reliable in past internationals?

Willie Pettigrew was just such a headache in 1976. He was on an incredible run of form for Motherwell, rarely missing a chance. Willie Ormond put him into the Scotland team for the first international of 1976 and it paid off. Pettigrew scored within two minutes to earn a 1-0 win.

Perhaps we'd be seeing more of Mr Ormond after all.

■ **Team v Switzerland, April 7th, 1976:**
1. **Alan Rough (Partick Thistle)**
2. **Danny McGrain (Celtic)**
3. **Frank Gray (Leeds United)**
4. **Tom Forsyth, captain (Rangers)**
5. **John Blackley (Hibernian)**
6. **Tommy Craig (Newcastle United)**
7. **Alex MacDonald (Rangers)**
8. **Kenny Dalglish (Celtic)**
    Sub, 64 min. Des Bremner (Hibernian)
9. **Willie Pettigrew (Motherwell)**
    Sub, 46 min. Bobby McKean (Rangers)
10. **Andy Gray (Aston Villa)**
11. **Derek Johnstone (Rangers)**

■ **Right: "Willie Willie Willie Willie Pettigrew"**
scores on his international debut.

Nutmeg

THE 1976 Scotland v England encounter is remembered for one thing – Kenny Dalglish nutmegging Ray Clemence to score the winner.

The nutmeg (to put the ball through your opponent's legs) is an odd thing in football. It sometimes doesn't achieve much but is a humiliation, a greatly significant thing to do (or have done to you), especially on a big occasion.

Ray Clemence, an accomplished goalkeeper with a trophy-laden career, is never – with no exception – mentioned in Scotland without a reference to being nutmegged at Hampden.

Scotland's equaliser in that game, a fantastic header by Don Masson, was by far the better goal. Masson had actually leaped too high to meet Eddie Gray's corner but showed great technique to bow in mid air and bullet his header into the top corner.

By contrast Dalglish, by his own admission, miskicked the shot that Clemence took his eye off (see next page).

Still, there is no mercy given or asked for in football. Great goal, lucky goal, miskicked goal – we won.

Nutmeg! Haw Clemence, ya mug ye!

■ **Right: That towering header by Masson (just out of shot) hits the net, to the consternation of Mick Mills, Ray Clemence, Mick Channon, and Kevin Keegan.**

■ Kenny shoots, and perhaps the strength (or lack of it) was deceiving. The ball bobbles along the turf and goes through Clemence's hands and then through his legs. Clemence (right) crumples in disbelief at what has just happened. The author of this book, for the record, lost a tooth in the North Enclosure when someone stood on his face in the vigorous, and drink-fuelled, celebrations that followed this goal! Great times.

Dark end to the Home Internationals

SCOTLAND were presented with the Home Internationals Trophy after the 1976 game.

The annual competition between Scotland, Wales, Northern Ireland and England was properly known as the British International Championship, and was the world's oldest international football tournament. It lasted exactly 90 years, 1894 to 1984.

The solid silver trophy, a winged figure atop a football, was given to King George V in 1935 by the Football Association to mark his silver jubilee. He, in turn, presented it to the Home Internationals to be the competition's trophy. It was first presented (to Scotland) in 1936 after a 1-1 draw at Wembley that left us top of the table by one point.

Scotland don't win many cups, but took this one outright on 24 occasions and shared it a further 17 times.

The competition came to an end with congestion in the football calendar cited as the main problem. But the rising tide of football violence in the 1980s was darkly mentioned as the real reason.

Organised English football "firms" travelled to Hampden for that last game in 1984, determined to challenge the oft-told legends of England supporters fearing to tread on Scottish soil.

There were further murmurs of what might happen the next time Scots hordes descended upon Wembley, the "turf" of England's most violent and most organised football thugs. Lurid stories spread of alliances being forged between London, Manchester, and Birmingham firms ready to battle the invaders.

In that final competition of '84, all four nations finished on three points. Throughout the tournament's history, goal difference (or goal average) was never taken into account, with the nations sharing the title if they were level on points.

On this last occasion, though, it was decided to bring in goal-difference. Northern Ireland, having scored three goals and conceded one, were declared the last ever winners and kept the trophy for all time.

It remains the centrepiece of the Irish Football Association's education and heritage centre at Windsor Park, Belfast.

■ **Team v England, May 15th, 1976:**
1. **Alan Rough (Partick Thistle)**
2. **Danny McGrain (Celtic)**
3. **Willie Donachie (Manchester City)**
4. **Tom Forsyth (Rangers)**
5. **Colin Jackson (Rangers)**
6. **Bruce Rioch (Derby County)**
7. **Kenny Dalglish (Celtic)**
8. **Don Masson (Queens Park Rangers)**
9. **Joe Jordan (Leeds United)**
10. **Archie Gemmill, captain (Derby County)**
11. **Eddie Gray (Leeds United)**
    Sub, 79 min. Derek Johnstone (Rangers)

■ Colin Jackson, Joe Jordan, Tom Forsyth, Kenny Dalglish, Alan Rough, and (front) Derek Johnstone and Danny McGrain with the Home Internationals trophy in 1976.

294

■ **Scotland v Sweden.** Asa Hartford's shot is punched on to the post by Swedish keeper Ronnie Hellstrom, but it rebounded, hit the unfortunate keeper, and went in. It was credited as an own-goal in the 3-1 win.

THE first international of 1977, a friendly against Sweden, was a very encouraging start to the year.

Kenny Dalglish was made captain for the first time, and Willie Johnston was recalled to the team after a seven-year absence. Ronnie Glavin, Joe Craig, and Dave Narey made their Scotland debuts.

Scotland looked fresh, an energetic and a potent side. The 3-1 win was well deserved.

However, it turned out to be Willie Ormond's last game as Scotland manager (see page 350).

(see page 350).

■ **Team v Sweden, April 27th, 1977:**
1. Alan Rough (Partick Thistle)
2. Danny McGrain (Celtic)
3. Willie Donachie (Manchester City)
4. Tom Forsyth (Rangers)
5. John Blackley (Hibernian)
   Sub, 76 min. Dave Narey (Dundee United)
6. Ronnie Glavin (Celtic)
   Sub, 58 min. Sandy Jardine (Rangers)
7. Kenny Burns (Birmingham City)
   Sub, 76 min. Joe Craig (Celtic)
8. Asa Hartford (Manchester City)
9. Willie Johnston (West Bromwich Albion)
10. Kenny Dalglish, captain (Celtic)
11. Willie Pettigrew (Motherwell)

Here we go, here we go

ALLY'S MACLEOD'S reign as Scotland boss (see page 352) started slowly. The squad had been picked by Ormond as his last act before leaving, although Ally would not – throughout his entire time in charge – introduce many new players to the team.

A 0-0 draw in Wales in the first of the year's Home Internationals was a bit of a surprise, although the Welsh would record a rare away win over England three days later – their first at Wembley since 1936.

Ally, meeting the Anglo-Scots for the first time before the Wales game, had introduced himself: "Hello, my name is Ally MacLeod, and I'm a winner."

Going against his natural attacking instincts, Ally had played a conservative game. The mistake wasn't to be repeated in the home encounter with Northern Ireland. Ally sent his team out to attack. Two Kenny Dalglish goals, and a Gordon McQueen header from a Masson free-kick gave Scotland a 3-0 win.

The scene was set for another great Wembley occasion.

Scotland would win the Home Internationals tournament for the second year in succession if they could beat England in London for the first time since the famous 1967 encounter.

■ **Team v Northern Ireland, June 1st, 1977:**
1. **Alan Rough (Partick Thistle)**
2. **Danny McGrain (Celtic)**
3. **Willie Donachie (Manchester City)**
4. **Tom Forsyth (Rangers)**
5. **Gordon McQueen (Manchester United)**
6. **Don Masson (Queens Park Rangers)**
7. **Bruce Rioch, captain (Everton)**
8. **Asa Hartford (Manchester City)**
9. **Willie Johnston (West Bromwich Albion)**
   Sub, 86 min. Archie Gemmill (Derby County)
10. **Kenny Dalglish (Celtic)**
11. **Joe Jordan (Leeds United)**
    Sub, 69 min. Lou Macari (Manchester United)

■ **Right: Pat Jennings gets a fingertip to another McQueen header in the Hampden win over the Irish.**

Their turf became our turf

WEMBLEY 1977 was both the high point, and the low point, of the traditional bi-annual Scottish invasion of London.

Scotland fans had, ever since the war, been proud to outnumber England fans at the old Empire Stadium, but there were never more tartan scarves inside Wembley than in 1977. Estimates put the Scots presence at up to 90,000 among the 100,000 crowd.

And Scotland took a deserved victory. Gordon McQueen was almost impossible to mark at set-pieces. Unlike many tall footballers he could jump as if rocket powered and possessed great timing. He would soon be transferred from Leeds to Manchester United for £500,000 – a record fee for a defender.

McQueen scored the opener with an awe-inspiring leap to get to a Hartford free-kick, before Dalglish doubled the lead in the second half. The late Channon penalty was barely noticed by many in the crowd.

Wembley didn't yet have crowd fences and as soon as the whistle went, Scotsmen poured on to the pitch. The ensuing scenes were, at the same time, funny, a great celebration, and would have dire repercussions.

Fences were put up at Hillsborough in 1977, so the disaster 12 years later can't be laid at the Scots' feet. Work on them was probably under way as this match went on. But it was scenes like these that persuaded many other club chairmen that fences were needed.

The weekend was used as further grounds for complaint from London's local politicians. They didn't like their boroughs being taken over by hordes of aggressive, very drunk Scotsmen.

The blazers of the FA didn't like their stadium being trashed either, and began to wonder if having the Scots visit every second year was actually a good thing.

This was the weekend of the Queen's Silver Jubilee, and London was bedecked in bunting, Union flags and a good proportion of windows were displaying pictures of the monarch. There was a lot less bunting, and many fewer Union Jacks, after the Scots had visited.

Again, it reads as a funny story. But these pieces of mischief, when added up, undoubtedly contributed to the fixture's demise.

Tragically, one Scots fan, Henry Low, of Edinburgh, died after attempting to dive into the fountain in Trafalgar Square, not knowing the water was only 15 inches deep.

■ **Right: Mick Channon had become the bogeyman in the English team, his every touch booed by Scotland fans. The Southampton striker was said to have made some harsh comments about Scotland, and Glasgow in particular, to earn his pantomime villain status. Gordon McQueen is pictured giving him a reminder to be more polite in future.**

ALLY MACLEOD had enjoyed a fantastic first few games as Scotland manager. We were in tartan heaven. The entire nation put their foot on the "wha's like us" accelerator. There weren't many who advised restraint, there weren't very many who even considered it. A train was in motion that couldn't be halted. For better or worse, we all signed up for the ride.

What followed was the most remarkable, fascinating, enjoyable – and unenjoyable – 12 months in Scottish football history.

■ **Right: Kenny Dalglish (almost hidden behind Phil Neal) scores what would turn out to be the winner at Wembley 1977, creating an explosion on the terraces. Today, young people call such celebrations "scenes". They may have invented the terminology, they certainly didn't invent the concept.**

■ **Team v England, June 4th, 1977:**
1. **Alan Rough (Partick Thistle)**
2. **Danny McGrain (Celtic)**
3. **Willie Donachie (Manchester City)**
4. **Tom Forsyth (Rangers)**
5. **Gordon McQueen (Leeds United)**
6. **Bruce Rioch, captain (Everton)**
7. **Don Masson (Queens Park Rangers)**
   Sub, 86 min. Archie Gemmill (Derby County)
8. **Kenny Dalglish (Celtic)**
9. **Joe Jordan (Leeds United)**
   Sub, 43 min. Lou Macari (Manchester United)
10. **Asa Hartford (Manchester City)**
11. **Willie Johnston (West Bromwich Albion)**

■ **The Wembley pitch invasion of 1977.**

TO this day, there are lawns in Scottish gardens that can boast they contain a little bit of Wembley turf brought home as a trophy.

"I was on the pitch in '77" is the ultimate credential for being a long-time Scotland supporter.

Ach, it was just a bit of fun, the crossbar got a wee bit dented but no one got hurt.

King Kenny

A FEW days after the fantastic Wembley win, the squad set off on a tour of South America in preparation for the World Cup in Argentina the following year – which we hadn't actually qualified for yet. Ally forced everyone to go, threatening any call-offs wouldn't be considered for the finals squad.

Kenny Dalglish was, at this point, reaching the height of his powers. He was 26, and on August 10th that year he signed for Liverpool after scoring 167 goals in 322 games for Celtic. The fee was £440,000, a British record at the time.

He would go on to be one of the best players ever to grace the English leagues, scoring a further 169 goals for the Anfield club and creating hundreds more for the likes of Ian Rush and John Aldridge.

Kenny was a genuinely world-class player, who would amass 102 caps and match Denis Law's total of 30 international goals.

Liverpool FC renamed their Kemlyn Road stand the Sir Kenny Dalglish Stand in 2017.

Scotland has never seen his like since.

■ **Kenny walks off the pitch of the Estadio Boca Juniors (the famed La Bombonera) in Buenos Aires on June 18th, 1977, having swapped shirts after Scotland drew 1-1 with Argentina in the South American familiarisation tour. This was the last Scotland international that was shown on UK TV only in black and white.**

Target Argentina

S COTLAND were in World Cup Qualifying Group 7, with familiar foes Czechoslovakia and Wales.

We lost away in Prague, but Wales beating the Czechs 3-0 at Ninian Park opened it up. Scotland knew they would qualify if they beat the Czechs at home, and Wales home and away. All winnable games, we reckoned.

Wales were seen off 1-0 at Hampden. Then the Czechs came to visit in September 1977.

And Scotland were superb that night – possibly the best full game performance since the Wembley Wizards half a century previously.

Jordan, Hartford, and Dalglish got the goals in a 3-1 victory.

It was there for all to see – we were one of the best teams in the world.

■ **Right: Joe powers home his header for the first, and (left) celebrates Kenny's goal.**

■ **Team v Czechoslovakia, September 21, 1977:**
1. Alan Rough (Partick Thistle)
2. Sandy Jardine (Rangers)
3. Danny McGrain (Celtic)
4. Tom Forsyth (Rangers)
5. Gordon McQueen (Leeds United)
6. Bruce Rioch, captain (Everton)
7. Don Masson (Queens Park Rangers)
8. Kenny Dalglish (Liverpool)
9. Joe Jordan (Leeds United)
10. Asa Hartford (Manchester City)
11. Willie Johnston (West Bromwich Albion)

THAT 1977-78 team had everything. They were street-wise, athletic, wily – and could play potent attacking football.

The back four was solid. Gordon McQueen and Tam Forsyth were composed but robust in the middle, and Scotland has never had a better full-back pairing than Jardine and McGrain.

The midfield four, Hartford-Masson-Rioch-Johnston, was a superb blend. Disciplined and creative in equal measure. They "clicked" as a unit.

Jordan and Dalglish was a clever front pairing. The ball could be played to them in any manner – a cross, a pass down the channels that they'd take facing or with their back to goal and furnish a chance.

McQueen and Jordan would give any team in the world a fright at set-pieces.

The Scottish football public are no mugs. We knew a good team when we saw one.

This wasn't a smoke-and-mirrors trick, it wasn't that Ally was trying to sell us snake oil. We all believed that this was, at long last, a Scotland team that could go places.

■ **The irrepressible Bud Johnston advises the ref that the Czech defensive wall isn't far enough back.**

A feral night in Liverpool

THIS was one of the most highly-charged nights in Scottish football history, indeed in World football history. This night, I assure, you, was incredible. There has never been an atmosphere like it at a football game in Britain. And, with standing at games and drinking banned, there never can be again.

The Welsh FA, with pound signs in their eyes, took the game away from the 14,000-capacity Ninian Park to Liverpool's 52,000-capacity Anfield.

Even then, the tickets scramble was unprecedented. The Welsh naively allowed postal applications for tickets to be sent to Scottish addresses, then made another mistake by putting tickets up for public sale in Cardiff. Long queues of Scots formed.

The official attendance was 52,000, but there were many more inside the ground.

Tens of thousands of Scots travelled without tickets and the scenes outside Anfield were reminiscent of a medieval castle siege, with rampaging northern tribesmen milling round the stadium trying to find weak spots to scale the walls. Some attempted to bribe (and often succeeded) turnstile operators to let them in. Some resorted to frontal attacks – charges by overwhelming numbers of tanked-up Scots broke exit gates at least twice, allowing thousands to pour in.

It was mayhem, a wild and supercharged night with an anything-can-happen feel to it.

Inside, especially on The Kop which was supposed to be for Wales supporters, there was lots of trouble. Bottles flew incessantly and the Welsh were almost squeezed out. It became Scottish territory.

Estimates vary, but many reckon there were about 7,000 Welsh supporters at what was supposed to be their home game, and 50,000 Scots.

The atmosphere as the game kicked off was tumultuous. The overstuffed terraces behind both goals were a beery, swaying, seething mass of Scotsmen.

The Scots expected their team to win, with the smell of blood on the wind if the result didn't go their way.

No game was ever played in a louder stadium.

And it turned out to be an end-to-end encounter. Searingly fast, tough as nails, with close things, great play, great saves, missed chances and (especially) bitter controversy. And Scotland won 2-0. Thankfully.

Football isn't like this any more. High-tech, all-seated stadiums have restricted movement and entry, and booze bans are tightly enforced. It had to change, of course. No one should ever be hurt at a game.

But the cost of safety was an end to incredible, intoxicating, feral nights like this.

■ **Right: the Welsh players complain (with good cause) to flamboyant French referee Robert Wurtz after he gave a penalty against them.**

LET'S be honest, it shouldn't have been a penalty.

If anyone handled the ball, it wasn't defender David Jones. But Don Masson coolly tucked away the spot-kick (left) amid scenes of carnage on all sides of Anfield.

A wonderful, flowing counter-attack saw Dalglish (pictured right) nod home a Martin Buchan cross for a clinching second late on.

Injuries had forced changes to the Scots from the last game, but every man on the park that night was a hero.

We were on our way to World Cup Argentina 1978.

What a time to be alive.

■ **Team v Wales, October 12th, 1977:**
1. **Alan Rough (Partick Thistle)**
2. **Sandy Jardine (Rangers)**
    Sub, 57 min. Martin Buchan (Manchester United)
3. **Willie Donachie (Manchester City)**
4. **Tom Forsyth (Rangers)**
5. **Gordon McQueen (Leeds United)**
6. **Asa Hartford (Manchester City)**
7. **Don Masson, captain (Queens Park Rangers)**
8. **Kenny Dalglish (Liverpool)**
9. **Joe Jordan (Leeds United)**
10. **Lou Macari (Manchester United)**
11. **Willie Johnston (West Bromwich Albion)**

Joe, a force of nature

JOE JORDAN was feart o' no thing and nobody. When you have an aggressive, powerful man on your side who leads by example, takes no prisoners, expects no mercy, and goes in where it really hurts – that spreads strength throughout the whole team.

Joe played the role of team example-giver for all of the club sides he played for. He went for crosses like a wolf goes for lambs – ferocious, hungry, lightning-fast.

Big Joe seemed indestructible. He was the toughest, meanest, most "gemme" player in a tough, mean period of football history when every player had to be "gemme" to survive.

THE early games of 1978 were very well attended – the fans all had World Cup fever. And for the players, there were seats on the plane to be had, and only a few games in which to stake a claim for one.

But the friendly with Bulgaria, in front of nearly 60,000, saw a few call-offs, so some new faces came into the reckoning.

■ **Team v Bulgaria, February 22nd, 1978:**
1. Jim Blyth (Coventry City)
2. Stuart Kennedy (Aberdeen)
3. Willie Donachie (Manchester City)
4. Willie Miller (Aberdeen)
5. Gordon McQueen (Manchester United)
6. Archie Gemmill, captain (Nottingham Forest)
7. Kenny Dalglish (Liverpool)
   Sub, 65 min. Ian Wallace (Coventry City)
8. Graeme Souness (Liverpool)
9. Joe Jordan (Manchester United)
   Sub, 65 min. Derek Johnstone (Rangers)
10. Asa Hartford (Manchester City)
11. Lou Macari (Manchester United)

■ **Team v Northern Ireland, May 13th, 1978:**
1. Alan Rough (Partick Thistle)
2. Sandy Jardine (Rangers)
3. Martin Buchan (Manchester United)
   Sub, 37 min. Kenny Burns (Nottingham Forest)
4. Tom Forsyth (Rangers)
5. Gordon McQueen (Manchester United)
6. Don Masson (Derby County)
7. Bruce Rioch (Derby County)
8. Archie Gemmill, captain (Nottingham Forest)
9. Joe Jordan (Manchester United)
   Sub, 46 min. Kenny Dalglish (Liverpool)
10. Derek Johnstone (Rangers)
11. John Robertson (Nottingham Forest)

■ **Liverpool's influential midfielder Graeme Souness, aged 25 at this point, won just his fourth cap in the 2-1 win over Bulgaria but did enough to take his place in the World Cup squad.**

■ Derek Johnstone won his 12th cap in the Home International against the Irish. He too would go to Argentina.

Never mind the minnows

FOR once, the England game wasn't the biggest date on Scotland's football calendar. We'd qualified for Argentina '78, they hadn't, so there wasn't really much notice being taken of what the minnows were up to as the world's big teams got ready for the more important event.

England won 1-0 with a late goal that was possibly a foul on Alan Rough, but were extremely lucky to do so. Scotland had most of the pressure and chances.

The crowd stayed on after the final whistle calling for the team to return to give a wave – which they duly did. It was one of the rare occasions in football that a lap of honour has been done by a beaten team, and certainly the only time such a thing has been seen after a Scotland defeat to England.

But the fans were confident and expectant. They wanted the lads to feel the support and love of the nation.

Despite the legends of submarines being hired and treks through the jungle, not many Scotland supporters travelled to Argentina. Only about 700 made it in those times of much more difficult (and very expensive) intercontinental travel. Very few fans from European nations went to South America – The Dutch had fewer than 100 there.

This was the last game most Scotland fans would see their heroes play before they watched them (on telly) meet Peru in Cordoba. It wasn't the last time they'd see the players, though. There was one more Hampden event to come (see page 322).

■ **Right: Great crowd, good team display, undeserved result. The author is 432nd from the left, row 94, in this pic. Easily picked out as he is wearing a tartan scarf.**

■ **Team v England, May 20th, 1978:**
1. **Alan Rough (Partick Thistle)**
2. **Stuart Kennedy (Aberdeen)**
3. **Willie Donachie (Manchester City)**
4. **Tom Forsyth (Rangers)**
5. **Kenny Burns (Nottingham Forest)**
6. **Don Masson (Derby County)**
   Sub, 74 min. Archie Gemmill (Nottingham Forest)
7. **Bruce Rioch, captain (Derby County)**
   Sub, 74 min. Graeme Souness (Liverpool)
8. **Asa Hartford (Manchester City)**
9. **Joe Jordan (Manchester United)**
10. **Kenny Dalglish (Liverpool)**
11. **Willie Johnston (West Bromwich Albion)**

The pool for 1978

IT's a who's who of 1970s Scottish football, and also a who's unlucky.

There was feverish speculation over who would be in, who would be out of the Argentina 40. Then renewed, probably even more feverish, speculation over who would make the final 22.

The provisional squad of 40 was made public in March, then the 22 was announced on May 3rd to play in the Home International games – to get used to each other and forge a team spirit – as well as the World Cup.

The biggest controversy (which only really became a widely discussed subject after the finals) was the decision to take Joe Harper but leave behind Andy Gray. Andy had enjoyed a spectacular three seasons since moving from Dundee United to Aston Villa, and had scored 29 in season 1977-78.

Joe was given only 17 minutes playing time in Argentina, as a sub for Kenny Dalglish in the Iraq game. Ally's detractors claimed he showed favouritism to the man who had been his striker at Aberdeen, but Joe had just completed a very good campaign too – scoring 27 goals.

Gray was sold to Wolves a year later for a then UK record fee of £1.49 million.

Don Masson and Bruce Rioch were both transfer-listed at Derby County, whose manager by then was none other than Tommy Docherty. County had narrowly avoided relegation from the English First Division. The Doc said it would benefit the two Scots midfielders to be "in the shop window" in Argentina.

Masson was eventually sold to Notts County, where he had played from 1968 to '74, and would stay for another four seasons. He later had the honour of being voted the club's best ever player by Magpies fans.

Rioch stayed at Derby for another year, but would have loan spells at Birmingham City and Sheffield United. The Doc left Derby in May 1979.

Of the famous names who had been in the 40, but didn't make the cut, it must be remembered that most of them were young. Willie Miller was 23, and would go on to amass 65 caps. But he had played only twice for the full Scotland side by summer 1978 and was often used as a midfielder in his early days.

Dave Narey would make the Scotland right-back slot his own in subsequent years but had only one cap (he would eventually get 35) by this point and was aged 22. Roy Aitken was only 19 and didn't make the first of his 57 Scotland appearances until 1979.

None of Roddie MacDonald, Neil McNab, George McCluskey, Tony Fitzpatrick, or Graeme Payne would ever be capped at full international level.

■ The squad record back-up vocals to the official World Cup song, Que Sera Sera, sung by Rod Stewart, who is present in cardboard cut-out form. Back, from left: Willie Donachie, Martin Buchan, Joe Jordan, Sandy Jardine, Derek Johnstone, Asa Hartford, John Blackley. Seated: Ally MacLeod, Bruce Rioch.

The final 22:

Goalkeepers
Jim Blyth (Coventry)
Bobby Clark (Aberdeen)
Alan Rough (Partick Thistle)

Defenders
Sandy Jardine (Rangers)
Stewart Kennedy (Aberdeen)
Willie Donachie (Manchester City)
Martin Buchan (Manchester United)
Tom Forsyth (Rangers)
Kenny Burns (Nottingham Forest)
Gordon McQueen (Manchester United)

Midfielders
Bruce Rioch (Derby County)
Don Masson (Derby County)
Asa Hartford (Manchester City)

Graeme Souness (Liverpool)
Archie Gemmill (Nottingham Forest)

Forwards
Lou Macari (Manchester United)
Joe Jordan (Manchester United)
John Robertson (Nottingham Forest)
Joe Harper (Aberdeen)
Kenny Dalglish (Liverpool)
Willie Johnston (West Bromwich Albion)
Derek Johnstone (Rangers)

In the 40 but didn't make the cut:

Goalkeepers
Jim Stewart (Middlesbrough)
David Stewart (Leeds United)

Defenders
Willie Miller (Aberdeen)

John Blackley (Newcastle United)
Dave Narey (Dundee United)
Paul Hegarty (Dundee United)
Roddie MacDonald (Celtic)
Frank Gray (Leeds United)

Midfielders
Neil McNab (Tottenham Hotspur)
Graeme Payne (Dundee United)
Tony Fitzpatrick (St Mirren)
John Wark (Ipswich Town)
Roy Aitken (Celtic)

Forwards
Andy Gray (Aston Villa)
Arthur Graham (Leeds United)
Ian Wallace (Coventry City)
Frank McGarvey (St Mirren)
George McCluskey (Celtic)

THIS is the legendary "celebration of winning the World Cup before we even left for Argentina" lap of honour at Hampden on the evening of Thursday, May 25th.

This event has had more misinformation and myths woven around it than almost any other happening in post-war Scottish football history.

It was not what it seemed.

See next page.

On the march with Ally's Army

ALLY MACLEOD was a confident, positive, inspirational manager. And that was a very good thing. Those are exactly the traits that are needed to be a successful football manager. He sent his players out of the dressing room convinced that they could win. It's the way Bill Shankly, Jock Stein, and Brian Clough sent out their teams – believing they could come out top in any game no matter who was the opposition.

But he wasn't so egotistical as to arrange the World Cup Gala Night (its official title) as a celebration of himself, or a presumption that his team would win the trophy.

The event was a collaboration between the SFA and Strathclyde Police that had the aim of gathering Scotland fans in one place that evening, where they could be more easily managed.

Everyone knew (it had been in all the papers) when the team were flying out. The police feared that fans would gather at the side of the roads and become a danger to themselves and traffic, crowding out on to the carriageways when the bus (or any bus) hove into view.

They also had anecdotal information that tens of thousands intended to gather at Prestwick Airport to cheer the lads off.

In the event, around 5,000 fans did actually show up at Prestwick and there were flag-waving fans at the side of roads out of Glasgow and all the way along the A77, but nothing like as much as there would have been.

And Hampden wasn't full, despite the photos (including these ones) you might have seen. The attendance was 22,732 (admission price was 30p) and fully half of the ground was closed.

After Argentina, Ally was unfairly criticised for dreaming up and staging the gala night.

He was, it must be said, a very visible figure in the months before the World Cup, he was constantly in the papers and on TV and radio. He appeared in several adverts and was even invited on to the BBC children's show *Blue Peter*, which was the height of stardom in those days.

It is the job of a football manager to promote his team. And Ally talked up his players whenever given a platform. It is a football fact that a team consistently referred to as "brilliant, winners, invincible," takes confidence, and a confident team is a good team.

And Ally didn't write Andy Cameron's fun single *Ally's Tartan Army*, which contained the lyric: "And we'll really shake them up, when we win the World Cup." But he was made to pay for those words.

The last thing Ally said to his wife Faye before boarding the plane for Argentina was: "I'll either come back a hero or a villain."

■ The players didn't want to take part in the gala night. They wanted to get on the plane for the 20-hour flight and were visibly embarrassed when called out, one by one, to the centre circle. They then had to carry an Argentina flag round the track before boarding an open-topped bus for another two circuits. There are only so many times you can wave to a crowd when you don't have a trophy as a centrepiecce of the celebration.

World Cup Argentina 1978

WE didn't win it. But we made quite an impression on the event.

Scotland were in Group 4, with Peru, Iran and the Netherlands.

We all know the story – so what went wrong?

A lot of things. As soon as the players got to their base in Argentina's second biggest city, Cordoba, in the foothills of the country's central Sierras Chicas mountains, they were cooped up in a soul-less, boring, prison camp-like compound for eight days. There was very little for them to do before the opening game.

From the start, as a result of the well-publicised Jimmy Johnstone in a rowing boat and Copenhagen Incident stories, the Argentinian press was obsessed with stories that depicted the Scots players as out of their minds on booze 24 hours a day. The local papers gave "eyewitness accounts" telling that the Scotland squad's luggage had included more than 30 cases of whisky (360 bottles), which was clearly nonsense.

But these fabricated reports led the image-conscious SFA to ban trips out of the camp in case any player was photographed drinking even a Coca-Cola.

The training facility was a 90-minute round-trip on a bus. There was supposed to be, as had been promised

■ **Archie celebrates "that goal".**

when the hotel was booked at the time of the draw, a full-sized training pitch right beside the hotel. But it was still a desolate piece of scrubland.

Phone calls home were next to impossible. The food was bland and repetitive. There was no water in the swimming pool. There was only Spanish language TV. Armed guards patrolled the perimeter fence.

There was discontent (as there often was in Scotland camps) at the SFA's intransigence over bonus payments. The players felt under-paid and under-appreciated, lonely, and cut off from the world.

These are all small things. Indeed, "no water in the pool" as an excuse for bad performances on the pitch is almost laughable. But they added up. It was a flat, humourless atmosphere. Morale plummeted.

Anyone who has been around a winning football team will tell you that success requires the group to be pulling together, all believing. Anyone who has been in an unhappy, despondent team will understand the weight, darkness, and lack of belief that descends.

However, while there are extenuating circumstances surrounding the accommodation and the discomforts, there can be no excuses. Let's not kid anyone, Scotland did not play well.

The three games each had their own problems.

The Peruvians – reigning Copa America champions

after all – were an awful lot better than anyone had anticipated.

Scotland had taken the lead through Joe Jordan and were, largely, giving as good as they got. Peru equalised and it was 1-1 at half-time.

We then got what was, to be fair, a very soft penalty. But Don Masson put it too close to the goalkeeper. Heads went down.

Then Teofilo Cubillas decided to start showing the world what can be done with the outside of the foot.

He first crashed a shot into the postage stamp from 25 yards, then scored what should be celebrated as one of the best free-kicks in history. He stroked a shot round the Scottish wall with an unorthodox stabbing motion that brought the outside of his right boot into connection with the ball. It looked effortless, a sublime football moment.

We lost 3-1.

The Scots had no time for admiring Cubillas, though. If things had gone badly on the pitch, they got much worse off it.

Willie Johnston failed a post-match drug test.

All he had taken was a cold remedy that was routinely dished out, and regarded as entirely safe, by his club West Brom. But he was treated as if he'd been caught mainlining heroin. The reaction was completely out of proportion.

Willie was hurriedly flown home, not even allowed farewells with his team-mates, to be met in London by overheated headlines proclaiming the "shame" of it all and a posse of hungry photographers.

Willie took it admirably. Many a Scottish footballer before and since would have lashed out at the cameras thrust in his face. There is footage of Willie being hassled on the plane to London that could be used as an archetypal illustration of press intrusion.

Looking back, it was ridiculous. But at the time this "drugs" story was an incredibly big deal.

To compound matters, Johnston's room-mate Don Masson claimed, then later retracted, that he'd also taken the cold remedy. It was possibly a loyal attempt to show solidarity with his friend but the SFA took fright and banned him from taking any further part in the World Cup. He wasn't sent home, however, as this would have caused another sensation.

Later, in a press interview after the Iran game, Lou Macari roundly criticised the SFA for the poor accommodation arrangements and he also became, quietly, a marked man never to play for Scotland again. But they didn't tell him this.

Back in Cordoba, the rest of the players were in a state that their mothers might describe as "affy doon in the mooth".

■ **Right: Ally's body language and facial expression say much about his feelings as he faces press questions after the loss to Peru.**

Rumours leaked through to them of the savaging they were getting in the press in the UK.

The flip side of being the only British side to qualify for the finals – and earning such close-focus from the newspapers – hit home. The English-based journalists let loose with the type of hateful vitriol they usually reserved for their own team when it failed at a big tournament.

What happened next was possibly the worst ever result by a Scottish team in a big game. We whimpered to a 1-1 draw with Iran.

The crowd for the Peru game had been around 38,000. The Iran game attracted less than 8,000.

While it was watched with feverish intensity live on TV in Scotland, the game itself was played out in front of an almost silent, apathetic crowd (apart from the small band of Scots supporters, who weren't exactly enjoying themselves!)

The goal Scotland scored was farcical. Iranian Andranik Eskandarian tucked away one of those "what on earth was he thinking?" own-goals that football throws up from time to time. Eskandarian went on to play for New York Cosmos, forming a solid defensive partnership with Franz Beckenbauer. The American scouts probably weren't at the Cordoba game.

The Iranians equalised with a shot from a narrow angle in the second half, after the Scots defence had four or five opportunities to clear their lines, or at least put in a mildly effective tackle. It is quite rare to see a goal scored in which every single player of a defence is, in turn, terribly at fault.

You could almost see the lack of confidence in the team.

If the reaction to the Peru loss was bad, things went thermonuclear after this game.

The press hyenas went for Ally's exposed throat in what was becoming a feeding frenzy.

Every aspect of Scotland's preparations, tactics and team selection was cut to pieces and a lot of people said "I told you so" who hadn't told us so at all. In fact they had actually told us the exact opposite just two weeks previously.

Ally's advertising contracts, his chat, his habitual facial expressions, even his appearance on *Blue Peter* was lambasted. It was deeply personal. He was shot in the head by football writers who had clapped their hands in coquettish delight at his every utterance mere days ago.

The treatment of Ally MacLeod is a shameful episode in Scottish football history, and the history of the British newspaper establishment.

There were calls made to his face, by journalists, for him to quit his job there and then after the Iran

■ **Right: The Tartan Army in mutinous mood as they gather beside the tunnel to jeer the players off the pitch after the Iran draw.**

game and fly home alone, just as Andy Beattie had done 24 years previously.

The nation scapegoated one man for a population's overblown optimism. Everything became his fault, just as Frank Haffey had been blamed for absolutely everything 17 years previously at Wembley.

Ally wasn't the only person who thought we'd do well in Argentina. We all thought we'd do well. Every single one of us. Every "expert" said we'd do well. And every football writer produced articles that took it as gospel that we'd do very well.

Conversely, in the game against The Netherlands, we then did do very well.

It is possibly the most "Scottish football" thing Scotland has done, over a long history of doing things the "Scottish football" way.

The team turned in a hard-running, creative, and skilled performance against the Dutch that included one of the best goals ever scored in a dark blue shirt.

A big part of the change was because the party relocated from Cordoba to Mendoza, a distance of just 400 miles, but which gave all the players the impression of a completely fresh start. A new, and better, hotel, a change of mood.

The gentlemen of the press had been suggesting we might get thrashed five or six by the Dutch, who were, it must be said, a very good side. They had beaten Iran 3-0, but then drew with Peru (two good sides cancelling each other out) in their second game.

Scotland's task was simple. To go level on points we needed to beat the World Cup finalists of 1974, the lauded "total football" masters.

And to take our goal-difference above theirs we had to do it by three clear goals.

It started badly. Kenny Dalglish "scored" after five minutes but it was disallowed because we weren't a big enough or fashionable enough nation.

Though we were playing well, with Souness and Gemmill running the midfield, Anderlecht winger Rob Rensenbrink scored a penalty just after the half-hour. But Dalglish rattled in a Jordan knock-down to make it level at half-time.

Whatever Ally said at half-time worked. Scotland came out like gunslingers. Suddenly, the swagger the team had shown the previous year was back, and the attacking verve also reappeared.

The Dutch contributed to the fun by hacking Graeme Souness down in the box, and Archie Gemmill tucked away the penalty.

Then it got even better. Dalglish was challenged and the ball broke back to Archie just outside the 18-yard box.

He rode a challenge from football common sense, a swivel of the hips took him past the balance of probability. He nutmegged the normal course of events and then, just as stark reality rushed out to close him down, he chipped the ball over the bounds of possibility and into the net.

All Scotland went daft.

There were 22 minutes left at that point. We needed one more goal to spit in the eye of every football expert who ever called themself a football expert.

However, the spittle dried on our lips just three minutes later when Johnny Rep strode forward and arrowed a 30-yard sickener into the top corner.

We were out of a World Cup. Again. Brave Scots go down fighting.

When looked at soberly, we could have won that last game by five or six and we still wouldn't have gone through to the next round.

FIFA had been pondering how to punish Scotland for the supposed drugs transgression, and if we'd beaten the Dutch their FA would have complained and hastened those ponderings. A points deduction had already been mentioned and would almost certainly have been imposed.

The squad flew home, arriving exactly three weeks since the Hampden Gala Night send-off.

The reception, from the fans at least, wasn't angry. A crowd of a few hundred applauded the team, and sang "We'll support you ever more".

There were positives from the Argentina experience although it took a while for them to show. Lessons were learned, on the pitch and off.

Organisation and administrative planning became much better for subsequent World Cups. The importance of getting the small things right was taken

■ **Team v Peru, June 3rd, 1978:**
1. Alan Rough (Partick Thistle)
2. Stuart Kennedy (Aberdeen)
3. Martin Buchan (Manchester United)
4. Tom Forsyth (Rangers)
5. Kenny Burns (Nottingham Forest)
6. Don Masson (Derby County)
   Sub, 70 min. Archie Gemmill (Nottingham Forest)
7. Bruce Rioch, captain (Derby County)
   Sub, 70 min. Lou Macari (Manchester United)
8. Asa Hartford (Manchester City)
9. Joe Jordan (Manchester United)
10. Kenny Dalglish (Liverpool)
11. Willie Johnston (West Bromwich Albion)

■ **Team v Iran, June 7th, 1978:**
1. Alan Rough (Partick Thistle)
2. Sandy Jardine (Rangers)
3. Willie Donachie (Manchester City)
4. Martin Buchan (Manchester United)
   Sub, 57 min. Tom Forsyth (Rangers)
5. Kenny Burns (Nottingham Forest)
6. Archie Gemmill, captain (Nottingham Forest)
7. Asa Hartford (Manchester City)
8. Lou Macari (Manchester United)
9. Joe Jordan (Manchester United)
10. Kenny Dalglish (Liverpool)
    Sub, 73 min. Joe Harper (Aberdeen)
11. John Robertson (Nottingham Forest)

■ **Team v The Netherlands, June 11th, 1978:**
1. Alan Rough (Partick Thistle)
2. Stuart Kennedy (Aberdeen)
3. Willie Donachie (Manchester City)
4. Martin Buchan (Manchester United)
5. Tom Forsyth (Rangers)
6. Archie Gemmill (Nottingham Forest)
7. Bruce Rioch, captain (Derby County)
8. Graeme Souness (Liverpool)
9. Joe Jordan (Manchester United)
10. Kenny Dalglish (Liverpool)
11. Asa Hartford (Manchester City)

into account. The importance of player happiness and team spirit was addressed.

And we were left to ponder another clutch of "what ifs". What if we'd gone to a World Cup straight after the incredible high of Wembley 1977? We peaked too early.

What if that World Cup had been in Europe? Scots would have made all the games "home" games.

What if the supreme motivator Ally had waited another five or 10 years before taking the national job? He'd never experienced an away tie in Europe as a manager and would have benefited greatly from staying at what was an up-and-coming Aberdeen side.

What if the bonus payments had been settled before leaving for the tournament? And the hotel had been all it promised to be, and the entertainment had been good, or the players' wives and girlfriends had been invited along – as would happen for later World Cups?

It would have been a different story.

The last word on Argentina must concern Ally MacLeod.

He wasn't sacked from the Scotland job.

The myth that has grown up around 1978 has it that he was axed, at the demand of a vengeful public, as soon as the plane landed.

But Ally was in charge for the next game, a Euro Qualifying tie against Austria in the September of 1978, that Scotland narrowly lost, 3-2 after being 3-0 down. We played well.

And then Ally walked away. It was his choice.

He was offered his old job as manager of Ayr United and despite taking a substantial pay cut he chose to return to a club that held only happy memories for him, that was on his doorstep, and that had always treated him well. He went back to the people who loved him.

Ally was in charge of Scotland for just 17 games.

■ As a post-script, that World Cup ended very badly for our group-mates Peru.

The second round of matches was also a group format. Argentina and Brazil were level on points in Group B going into the final round of matches. But hosts Argentina somehow managed to have their game against Peru delayed a few hours, so they knew what they had to do to get through to the final.

Brazil beat Poland 3-1, meaning the host nation had to get past Peru by four goals. It was 2-0 Argentina at half-time, but the Peruvians barely kicked a ball or attempted a tackle in the second half and eventually (amid many accusations) lost 6-0.

Imagine if Ally's Scotland had done that!

■ Right: Gaun yersel wee man! Archie Gemmill is just about to clip the ball over Dutch keeper Jan Jongbloed to score "that goal".

The managers of Scotland

IT'S certainly not an easy job to be manager of your country's football team. The pressures are like those of a club manager, but magnified several times.

Everyone in the country thinks they can do the job better than you. Every newspaper, before every game, will be full of "experts" telling you who to pick for the team, and the formation to play.

After the game, page upon page will be dedicated to your failings. All the reporters will ask what you think, but none will care how you feel.

You will play "friendlies" but they aren't friendly at all, and they all count on your win-loss record.

You have to qualify for major tournaments, and beat teams ranked higher than yours, or lose your job.

To make matters worse for the Scotland manager, until 1967 you didn't even get to pick the team. SFA "selectors" did this for you. Mere administrators who had worked their way through the Scottish Football Association hierarchy but who weren't professional football men. It was ludicrous. Who leaves team selection to factory owners and haulage contractors?

For many years, the national job wasn't seen as a full-time position. And the man in charge had to also manage the Under-23 and Scottish League teams.

And the pay wasn't very good either, club jobs were much more lucrative.

The management history of Scotland is patchy. There wasn't a manager in the real sense of the word for many years, but Andy Beattie was engaged on a part-time basis in 1954 (although he didn't last long, see page 48). Then Matt Busby was to be part-time manager for the 1958 World Cup, until he was badly injured in the Munich Air Disaster.

Andy returned, again part-time, briefly in 1959.

However, over the years that are the scope of this book (the war until 1978), these were the men who held the post:

Ian McColl, part-time (1960-65)

Jock Stein, interim part-time (1965)

John Prentice, part-time (1966)

Malky MacDonald, caretaker (1966-67)

Bobby Brown (1967-71)

Tommy Docherty (1971-1972)

Willie Ormond (1973-77)

Ally MacLeod (1977-78)

Each did the job differently. Each had his own challenges to face.

But for all the slings and arrows, it is a job only given to the very best in the land. It is a great honour to manage the Scotland team.

■ The 19-year-old Ally MacLeod (centre) with his Third Lanark team-mates Jim Baird and Willy Vandermotten, in 1950. Ally would get the Scotland manager job 27 years later.

Ian McColl

SCOTLAND had a succession of part-time and caretaker managers in the 1950s and though this system never worked very well there was no "lightbulb moment" that made the SFA realise they should have a permanent man.

Ian McColl was announced as boss on November 3rd, 1960, but it was on a game-by-game basis. Throughout his five-year reign – although his position was eventually recognised as a long-term arrangement – he remained part-time.

Ian was the last member of Rangers' fearsome "Iron Curtain" defence to retire from playing and was widely respected in the game.

He was still registered as a player with Rangers, although at age 33 at the time of his Scotland appointment he hadn't featured in Rangers' first-team since the previous season's Scottish Cup Final. He had played for Scotland as recently as 1958.

Ian had a Home International at Hampden against Northern Ireland on November 9th, 1960, as his first task –

■ **Ian McColl argues with Dutch referee Leo Horn during the Scotland v England game at Hampden in 1964.**

with a team picked by the SFA selection committee. It was a 5-2 win (Scotland's first victory in eight games), with debutant Ralph Brand, Ian's former team-mate at Rangers, scoring two.

The second of Ian's matches, five months afterwards, was the infamous 9-3 defeat at Wembley (see page 90).

There was talk after that about Ian's inexperience as a manager, but he overcame the bad start to win the Home International Championships in 1962 and 1963.

His stats show that he won 17 of the 28 matches in which he managed the side, just over 60% – the best winning ratio of any Scotland manager until Alex McLeish's 10-game first spell in 2007.

Ian was asked to resign after a 2-2 draw with England at Wembley in 1965, followed by a dull 0-0 with Spain at Hampden. England had been reduced to effectively nine men for the second half after injuries, but Scotland couldn't find a winning goal.

The selectors, who had picked the teams for both games, decided they had "no confidence in him".

Ian quickly became Sunderland manager at a salary six times what Scotland had been paying.

Jock Stein

JOCK'S second spell as manager of Scotland is better remembered than his first in 1965. He was 44, and the "hot" manager in Scotland. He'd turned Dunfermline into a trophy-winning side, reinvigorated Hibs, then arrived at Celtic Park and would almost immediately win the Scottish Cup. His team was playing exciting, attacking football that anyone could see was going to bring results.

The Celtic board only agreed to his temporary and part-time appointment to the Scotland job if it didn't interfere with his club duties.

Though the selectors were still in place, Stein made it clear to the SFA that he alone selected the team.

The task was clear: qualify for the 1966 World Cup, with five qualifying ties to do it in. A home defeat to Poland effectively killed the chances of that, but the home and away games with Italy (see page 156) brought unprecedented excitement to the national team.

Stein stepped away from the job after the Italy game in Naples, and those close to him whispered that he regretted ever taking it on. He hadn't liked working with the SFA and their committee one bit, and was baffled by the practice of taking 11 players to away games with just one travelling reserve.

■ **Left: Jock emerges from the SFA headquarters at Park Gardens having agreed to take on the job.**

■ **Right: April 1965. Jock takes his first training session with the squad at Largs.**

342

■ Matt Busby had been part-time Scotland boss in the late 1950s.

MALKY MACDONALD took the Scotland job as caretaker, on a part-time basis, in 1966. He had played for Celtic, Kilmarnock and Brentford and had managed Killie and (with great success) Brentford, and was again the boss at Rugby Park when the Scotland call came.

He was only in charge for two games, against Wales and Northern Ireland. But delivered a very impressive 3-1 Scottish League win over an English League side that contained several members of the side who would lift the World Cup a few months later.

A side-effect of this win was an almost unanimous call in the Scottish press for Scotland full international teams to include only home-based players.

Scotland had had a short period in the 1920s when only home-based players were selected and that was well within living memory.

This resulted in added antipathy from the crowd towards Anglo-Scots which was prevalent for several years to come.

Despite being a Kilmarnock great, MacDonald is one of those highly-accomplished Scottish football men who deserves greater recognition than he ever got in his home country.

He is a member of the Brentford FC Hall of Fame.

John Prentice

A S a player, John Prentice had a good career with Rangers and captained Falkirk's 1956 Scottish Cup-winning side. He cut his management teeth with Arbroath then moved on to Clyde, winning them promotion followed by a seventh-placed finish in the 18-team First Division.

He was announced as the new Scotland manager on March 25th, 1966, with a contract until after the World Cup of 1970.

The selectors had issued an 18-man pool of players for the Home International clash with England, which was less than a week away. It was said that the manager would have the "final say" on the make-up of the team. Times were changing, but the selection committee was clearly still operating.

Scotland lost 4-3 to England, and the next game was a 3-0 loss to The Netherlands, who had only part-time players at the time. It was described as a great embarrassment for Scotland.

Then came two friendlies that provided World Cup warm-ups for Portugal and Brazil (see pages 170 and 172). Scotland had drawn one and lost three of Prentice's games.

After a personal trip to Canada there were reports that John had been offered the job as manager of Vancouver FC. There had been no negotiations, just an offer.

The SFA, however, asked John to resign and when he didn't they put out a statement saying they had "dispensed with the services of Mr Prentice", on the grounds they should have been told he was looking for another job. There were widespread rumours this was just an excuse to get rid of him.

■ **Right: John Prentice (back, left) with the Scotland pool at the North British Hotel in Glasgow before the 1966 game against England.**

Bobby Brown

IT took several months before a new manager was found, with Malky MacDonald, still the Kilmarnock boss, again in place as caretaker. The SFA invited applications but then offered the job to Bobby Brown, who had been St Johnstone boss for nine years but hadn't applied.

Bobby had been an international goalkeeper, after making his debut for Queen's Park while he was still at school. He went on to be another member of the Rangers Iron Curtain, playing 10 years at Ibrox 1946-56.

He was announced as Scotland manager on February 27th, 1967, and had full control of player selection. However, the selection committee remained in place to assess players and help keep admin staff busy with their expenses claims.

To say the old way of working was outdated is a comical understatement. The committee compiled lists of full-backs, right-halfs, left-wingers, etc. Three or four candidates for each position. Then they voted on which player might slot in to each shirt. Little consideration was given to new-fangled notions such as altering formation.

Bobby was in the Scotland job for four years, but didn't manage to qualify for The Euros of 1968, or the World Cup of 1970. He did, however, steer Scotland to that famous 1967 win at Wembley.

His removal, unlike that of many Scotland managers, was a civilised and orderly affair after a bad run of results in the early months of 1971.

■ **Blond-haired Bobby, nicknamed "The Golden Boy" when at Ibrox, was always a gentleman, even when speaking to the press.**

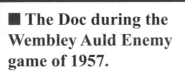

■ The Doc during the Wembley Auld Enemy game of 1957.

Tommy Docherty

THE Doc had been a Scotland stalwart as a player. He won 25 caps over eight years, 1951-59, captained the team 11 times, and went to two World Cups.

His career started at Celtic, though he played only nine games. He then turned out 324 times for Preston North End before a big-money transfer to Arsenal.

He had succeeded Bill Shankly as right-half at Deepdale, and was a tough, uncompromising, and always very fit midfielder who played a major role – alongside the great Tom Finney – in the North End side.

Tommy was announced as Scotland manager on September 12th, 1971, initially as an "interim appointment" as he was still also boss of Hull City.

Having spent many years down south he brought in a lot of Anglos, his first squad of 16 contained nine players with English clubs. Four made debuts against Portugal.

But Scotland prospered under the reign of the confident, charismatic Doc, the players benefiting from his ability to create a club spirit. We were well on our way to qualification for the 1974 World Cup. It might be said this was the high point of Tommy's lengthy career – international management suited his personality.

Then, on December 16th, 1972, Crystal Palace beat Manchester United 5-0 at Selhurst Park and the Red Devils sacked Frank O'Farrell. General Manager Sir Matt Busby had a word in Tommy's ear (a large salary was mentioned) and The Doc left Scotland after just 14 months in the job.

Willie Ormond

WHO would it be this time? Hearts boss Bobby Seith, Nottingham Forest manager Dave Mackay, and Davie McParland, who was in charge of Partick Thistle, were all considered. But, as with Bobby Brown, the SFA eventually looked to Perth for their new man.

Willie Ormond had been a member of the renowned Hibs Famous Five forward line of the 1950s. He became assistant trainer at Falkirk after his playing career ended in 1962, then succeeded Brown as St Johnstone boss in 1967.

Donny was announced as boss on January 5th, 1973. A more reserved man than the ebullient Doc, he suffered a difficult start as Scotland boss. But he recovered well and the performances on the way to, and during, the 1974 World Cup were among the best in our nation's football history.

However, in May 1977 Hearts had just been relegated for the first time ever and, determined to quickly fight their way back into the Premier League, needed a new manager. They offered Willie a substantial increase on his Scotland salary.

Willie had just enjoyed a fairly good run as Scotland boss, but the desire for a new manager had been openly discussed by SFA men a scant few months previously after the Copenhagen Incident (see page 284). Willie clearly didn't felt secure in the Scotland hot seat. He took the Hearts job.

■ **Left and right: Willie Ormond loved the game. He had been a gifted player and never passed up a chance to have a kick-about. He is seen here with his former Famous Five team-mate Eddie Turnbull (Aberdeen manager at the time) during a coaching course at Largs in 1969. Just twa fitba-daft old friends kicking a ba'.**

Ally MacLeod

THE first name the press seized upon to fill the vacant post was Bill Shankly (pictured left). The Liverpool legend was 64 and had been out of work for three years, but if anything his reputation had grown in that time.

It turned out to be wishful thinking. But the notion of Shanks as Scotland boss remains an intriguing "what if?"

Dave Mackay, by then Derby County boss, was still being tipped, as was Jock Stein, again. But Celtic issued a statement saying Jock wasn't moving.

So Ally MacLeod (right) who was just 18 months in-post at Aberdeen but who had already won a trophy, emerged as favourite. He was unveiled as the new boss at a press conference at Park Gardens, on Wednesday, May 18th, 1977.

Ally told the reporters present: "I want to prove that I am the best manager in the world. People might laugh at that, but I firmly believe I was born to be a success."

The story of his time in charge has already been told in this book, but a couple of aspects of his career and character deserve to be highlighted. Ally was maligned (following Argentina 1978) for possessing little big game experience, having not been an international player himself, or ever managed a club in a European tie.

But his playing career was impressive. He was a flying left-winger and, as a Blackburn Rovers star, the 1960 FA Cup Final's man of the match. He knew about big games.

Further, he was a man of honour. In a pay dispute in 1963 Ally decided to leave Blackburn for Hibs. At the last moment Blackburn said they would better the money Hibs were paying. Ally wanted to stay in Lancashire, but felt that because he had accepted Hibs' offer he couldn't go back on his word.

Who was the best Scotland player of the black & white era?

AS we near the end of this book, it is a fair question to ask, though certainly not an easy one to answer. How do you measure such things?

Going back a long way, Hughie Gallacher was a quite incredible footballer. An auld fitba heid told me, nearly 40 years ago, that Gallacher was the Diego Maradona of his era – but faster, two-footed, better in the air, and a lot tougher. Few remember Hughie's last game for Scotland in 1935. Still fewer saw him in his prime, scoring five in one game against Northern Ireland in 1929.

Slim Jim Baxter and Jinky Jimmy Johnstone would also be candidates for the title of the most naturally skilfull player to pull on a Scotland shirt.

The most accomplished all-round footballer would be Kenny Dalglish. He could do everything.

But being the best ever Scotland player is about a little bit more than football talent. Attitude has to be taken into account, and there has to be a measure of the archetypal Scottish character in there too.

Denis Law hated losing. Bremner had such a mentality too, as did George Young. But Denis brought goals with his desire to triumph. That one-arm-raised salute, with sleeve cuff held in hand, was seen 30 times in 55 games. And he relished a physical challenge on the pitch – take a look at his battle with Germany's Franz Beckenbauer in the 1969 World Cup qualifier at Hampden.

Denis was a sinuous, lithe athlete. He was supreme in the air. He contorted like a spring when he jumped, uncoiling to get power into headers in a way that was unique to him. Take a look at his goal against England at Hampden 1966.

And he couldn't be intimidated. Kick him once, he'd tell you (in no uncertain terms) not to do it again. Kick him twice and he'd kick you back. Harder. If you wanted to engage in further argument about it, Denis would finish that argument for you.

The Lawman didn't hold back.

He went for the ball as if his life depended upon it, and expected defenders and goalkeepers to do the same. If such an approach resulted in physical pain (and it often did) it was better than the mental anguish of being second best.

Denis is a proud Aberdonian (he has done a lot of charitable work in the city) and a proud Scot.

And he wasn't given the nickname "The King" for nothing.

■ A break from training at Largs in 1967.

We'll support you ever more

SCOTLAND players are heroes. Every one of them. Their names go down in history. They will be feted for ever not just as "Hamish McTavish, football player", but "Hamish McTavish, SCOTLAND INTERNATIONAL."

And it is, of course, the highest accolade a player can be given. To be so good at the game we all try to be good at that you are picked to represent your country. That's quite something.

A Scottish football international doesn't even require his or her sport to be identified. If you describe them as "played for Scotland", that's enough. All other sports need "at badminton/darts/rugby/tiddlywinks" explanation attached.

We Scots perfected the modern game and took it to all corners of the world.

However, along with the immortality and adulation several other things come to a Scotland player.

These players are for ever judged to a higher standard than others who step on to a football pitch.

They are still heroes but their every stumble, every minor mis-control, or missed chance – in every game – might be subject to a wry nod and the harshly sarcastic: "A Scotland player? Oh aye."

Worse, if they have been present for one of our fairly regular defeats and debacles, blame is attached to them no matter what part they played. These scapegoats are sacrificed on the national high altar of disappointment – and the shame lasts for all time. Even their sons, daughters and grandchildren will be tainted with a shadow.

So why would anyone want to play for Scotland? History would appear to have proved that the folly of taking part in a simple game with a ball while wearing a dark blue shirt can only end in pain and defeat.

But we play, and would elbow aside others in our passion to play, because football is our love and our life, our moon and our stars. Our morning, noon and night. Football is our oxygen.

Would a Scot rather win a million pounds or score a World Cup-winning goal? If you choose the money, then choose another place to live because you aren't truly Scottish.

We play because one day it will all come right.

One day we will put a team on the park that is the essence of Scotland. Our spirit, our birthright, our best, our brightest. One day we will fulfill our potential. One day we will rule the world.

We have a dream, and one day that dream will come true.

■The team for the first game of the World Cup Finals of 1958, v Yugoslavia (see page 60), probably pictured at Hamilton Park, Girvan, before leaving for Sweden. Back, from left: John Hewie, Eric Caldow, Tommy Younger, Eddie Turnbull, Bobby Evans, Doug Cowie. Front: Graham Leggat, Jimmy Murray, Jackie Mudie, Bobby Collins, Stewart Imlach.

The way an accurate caption for this photo was found was to consult the professors of the Old Scottish Football Pictures group on Facebook. My thanks, and admiration, goes to them.

The best collection of football knowledge is held in the most valuable information repository in existence: the memories of those who saw it all happen.